lighthouse revolution

stand tall. light up. shine bright.

karen gunton

karengunton.com

copyright © karen gunton 2016

ISBN 978-0-9945646-0-3

editing: assisi chant assisichant.com

cover design: karen gunton

cover image: CC0 public domain pixabay.com author: skeeze

author photo: kelli dudley kellidphotos.com

formatting: ebooklaunch.com

printed by: ingramspark.com

table of contents

about this book

as you will notice right away, this book does not contain capital letters. i share the full story about this choice later on in the book, but right now you are probably wondering what the hell is up with that?

when i started writing and blogging in 2010 i really struggled at first to get my words on the page and nothing i wrote felt like me because i was trying to conform to all the rules i had in my head about writing. i decided then and there to just be me. to write like i talk, to swear if i want to, and to not use capital letters. once i gave myself permission to be me, and to break the rules, the words started to flow.

since that day you will not find a capital letter in anything i write, teach, create, or share. ever. any-where. including this book. (well, unless i am doing SHOUTY caps. i like those caps.)

so, if i started using capital letters now - just be-cause this is not a blog post or a social media image but a real book book, one printed on actual paper with a glossy cover and everything - well that would be a complete cop out wouldn't it?

my message has always been that you need to be YOU. just as i need to be me. the whole premise of building a lighthouse is that you deserve to own your light in the world and live a life that lights you up... it all starts with being you, and honouring who you are, and lighting up in whatever way you choose.

and so i will carry on shining my light in the way that feels like me, and i hope to inspire you to do the same.

now let's make like a lighthouse and shine...

introduction

i believe that we are each here for a reason. we each have a purpose - a soul's purpose - that we are meant to find and fulfil and share with others... something we are meant to discover about ourselves and truly *BE* as ourselves... a journey we are meant to take.

we are each here to shine our light in this world.

in whatever way we choose, in whichever way calls to us.

but damn it can be a tough road to take!

i've been on this journey for a long time now, and i will completely admit that this whole 'shining my light' thing is definitely not as easy as i thought it would be.

"follow your passion" they said.

"do what you love" they said.

"just take a leap" they said.

and yes, those are certainly some good places to start.

but what no one said is that there is much more to the story... much more that we need to build in our lives and in ourselves, if we truly want to shine.

this book is about the rest of that story.

turning points

can you pinpoint a moment in your life that everything changed for you?

i often look back on my business journey and say that the moment that someone asked *"how much do you charge?"* was the moment that changed everything... it was the first time i ever considered that i could actually build my own business.

but really, my journey started much earlier... like most people, i have had a long and winding road to arrive at where i am right now.

15 years ago i was starting my hard-earned career as a middle school science teacher, in edmonton, canada. and i loved my job, i loved teaching, and for a long time i couldn't imagine not being a teacher. my work was everything.

and then i had a baby. and of course then i realized that what i thought was 'everything' was hardly anything at all! suddenly my heart was bigger than i thought possible and my whole worldview had shifted.

it was while i was on maternity leave that i began to feel the whisper of an idea that i wasn't actually meant to be a school teacher forever, that perhaps there were other things out there for me to create and learn and teach and experience.

at that time i was staying at home with my seven month old baby, and my hubby and i (in a moment of madness) thought it would be a good idea to live in a caravan for the summer. it was a bit miserable.

all of my old friends and family would probably chuckle reading this, because they could picture us there on the outskirts of town, in the middle of a miserable alberta winter... errr i mean summer (but truthfully, it is basically the same thing for this part of canada).

i always tell the story that my hubby came home from work one day - and i was hiding from the rain and chill, trapped inside a caravan with a baby learning to crawl, feeling isolated and freaking bored out of my mind.

he said: "what do you think about moving to adelaide, australia? i want to go to medical school there; they have an awesome international program."

and the story goes that i googled *adelaide* - saw the average temperature and sunshine - and said HELL YES. (he was prepared to have to convince me and never even got to try out his long list of thoughtful arguments!)

i also said yes because i knew it was my hubby's dream to become a doctor and i never wanted him to regret not following that path... i never wanted to be the person who stood in the way of his dreams.

but there is one more reason i said yes. one that i haven't admitted to many people.

saying yes to australia was my version of running away.

deep down i did not want to go back to work full time... which i would have had to do in just four short months! my teaching career no longer called to me, as it once had. but i also didn't want to be a full-time stay at home mum either. i knew i needed something of my own, something more to feel fulfilled and fired up.

so i felt a bit lost. i had identified as a 'teacher' for so long, the thought of just walking away from that (and everything i had been working towards) scared me.

there was no one in my circle who didn't go back to work after maternity leave. it was unheard of, so i felt like i was in uncharted waters. in my world you didn't just give up your career! you didn't just change careers either! and you certainly didn't talk about a tiny little niggling feeling that maybe you were called to do something else.

you went on maternity leave. and then you went back to work. and maybe you had a few more babies and breaks, and maybe even went part time until your kids were older. and then you worked as a teacher until you retired with a pension.

done and dusted.

i wanted something else out of life, but i had no idea what it was, or how to find it.

so when hubby said *"do you want to go?"* i think somewhere deep inside i immediately saw my escape.

i didn't have to decide. i didn't have to figure it out. i didn't have to be afraid of what would happen if i didn't go back to my career. or worse, what would happen if i did!

that moment - that 'yes' - was the true start of my biz journey. mind you, it was still another three years before i actually started my own business, and at that time i certainly had no thought of ever, ever starting a biz (if you had have asked me then, i would have thought the idea was crazy!)

in that moment i had no idea what door i just opened or where it would take me. all i knew was that it gave me an out, so i took it.

without realizing it, that 'yes' offered me some space. it gave me permission. it opened up possibility.

to explore who i was now... not just a teacher, not just a mum, not just a wife, not quite the same as the old karen that i once was.

to explore my passions besides teaching... which ironically brought me right back to teaching! (a soul journey is a truly fascinating thing!)

and to explore what i came here to do, what i was born to do.

i sometimes wonder what would have happened if i said NO to australia. i imagine my soul would have tapped me on the shoulder in some other way, and eventually i would have found my path.

eventually you have to give in to the call.

as much as you try to ignore it, those niggling feelings will just grow stronger and the tapping on the shoulder will eventually turn into bashes over the head... in one way or another!

what is whispering inside you right now? in what way is your soul calling out to you?

whether you are longing to make a change, longing to explore a part of you that is hiding inside, longing to find yourself again, longing to put something new into the world, longing to finally try that thing you've been wanting to try...

maybe this is your moment.

maybe you have had other moments too, other sign posts on your journey. it's worth thinking about... they all add up to something.

what are you here to do? how will you choose to spend your life?

ah ha moments

i don't know for sure what life would be like for us if we had stayed in canada - it's one of those 'sliding doors' moments, where one decision builds a completely different life than the other decision does.

i am guessing that that life probably would have been just as happy as this one is. and eventually i would have had to listen to that whisper that was calling me to other things - that sort of whisper doesn't let up.

but what i do know for sure is that that choice opened a little door for the next steps on my journey.

once we moved to adelaide i did not miss my teaching job but i certainly missed having something all my own. i missed learning and planning and dreaming and creating. i missed connecting with like-minded teachers. i missed having my own money in my pocket!

and so i accidentally started a photography business.

i say *accidentally* because i had no clue about starting a business, i had no plan, i had no idea what i was doing. but someone asked me how much i charged and i went for it - another of those 'sliding doors' moments that changed everything.

so photography became my part time business and learning about business became my full time job. i suppose it is the teacher in me - i tackled learning business like i would any subject, with passion and fervour, learning everything i could and flipping it around in my brain until it all clicked.

after 2 years of building my photography business i started a little blog on the side to share with others what i had been learning about business. my blog, *build a little biz*, grew to be very popular and my photography business was going well - things were great!

until they weren't.

my circumstances changed once again with my husband's schedule becoming more and more gruelling. i now had three kids to take care of, including a new baby boy, and somewhere along the way i had lost my mojo... to tell the truth, i didn't even want to get out of bed most days.

i had a very popular blog that wasn't making much money. i had a successful photography business that didn't fit my life any more. i wasn't particularly passionate about either one at this point and wasn't sure what to do next.

it was a pretty bleak time actually. i was tired all the time. i was pretty blue. and i felt like i had lost myself again, along with that mojo.

at that time i was surfing around on pinterest, as you do when you are 'working' but actually you are procrastinating, and i came across this quote from anne lamott:

"lighthouses don't go running all over an island looking for boats to save; they just stand there shining."[1]

when i read that quote i had one of those ah ha moments that you know are important even as they are unfolding... the kind that come with goose-bumps.

in that moment i knew *that* was what i wanted for myself.

i didn't want to build a business or a blog... i wanted to build a lighthouse.

i could picture, in my mind's eye, women and businesses that epitomised the lighthouse... standing tall, standing out... standing there shining bright.

i wanted *that*.

and so began a quest to figure out what it means to shine.

i got back to me. i got back to what got me started in business in the first place. i got my mojo back. i found my spark - that sweet spot of finding your passion and purpose and doing what lights you up.

i shut down my photography business. i turned my side blog into my full time business. i started teaching again... teaching women in business about branding and marketing and visual content creation.

and everything was awesome.

until it wasn't again.

well that's not fair to say. it's not that things weren't awesome, they were. but i still felt like something was missing.

i was ticking the boxes, doing all of the things that everyone says you need to do in order to have a successful business but i still felt like there was a missing piece of the puzzle that i was *just. not. getting.*

it felt like i was missing the heart and soul of the business.

it felt like i was missing a secret ingredient that would make my work feel more purposeful.

it felt like i was missing the piece that would really make a difference in the world.

at that time i was doing an interview with someone who would come to be a great friend. she was doing a series of videos with tips and ideas for women in biz and i was sharing the story of the lighthouse quote and how it changed everything for me and my business.

after the interview, my friend said to me: "you have to talk about the lighthouse."

i had been talking about what it means to 'shine' for 2 years by then, talking about the idea of finding your spark, and being YOU. i replied, "i *am* talking about this stuff!" but she said, "nope, there is something more to share about the *lighthouse*. i don't know what it is, or what it will do, i just know that talking about the lighthouse is the key to opening the next door on your journey."

my friend is highly intuitive, so when she says i ought to explore something, i listen!

and so i started blogging about the lighthouse as a symbol for the business that i wanted to build. i shared my story. i allowed myself to be vulnerable and raw and open. and i was blown away by the response.

the lighthouse resonated.

and so i began to ask myself: what else can i learn from the lighthouse? i had already learnt so much about what it means to 'shine' but i thought: maybe there is indeed, more to the story.

you see, my brain works in an interesting way. i love to figure out how the pieces of the puzzle all fit together. i love to follow the clues and the signs. i love to find meaning in things. and i love to move the pieces around until everything clicks. i *really* love to make things click, not just for myself but for others, through teaching and writing.

and so began the lighthouse revolution.

a quest to find out if there was indeed more to the story... if there was a better way to build the sort of life that i wanted for myself. one with success but also with heart and soul. one that would allow me to be on purpose and feel lit up from within.

i figured that if i wanted to shine my light in the world the best thing to do would be to build myself a freaking lighthouse.

right?

because as i have discovered, the lighthouse doesn't suddenly, magically appear just because you decide that now is the time to shine. you've got to build it yourself. you've got to decide to BE it for yourself.

a revolution

when i first began to explore the symbol of the lighthouse and what we could learn from it, i considered calling this work a variety of different things: the lighthouse project, the lighthouse process, the lighthouse method, the lighthouse strategy...

but in the end i settled on the lighthouse revolution. why revolution?

because i believe it is time for transformation. for me, this has been about changing the way i think about the life that i am building... transforming my thoughts, beliefs, and actions so that i can better live a life that truly lights me up.

to be part of a revolution means doing things differently. we need to stop just going through the motions in life - being content with the slow incremental changes of evolution - and instead create purposeful, meaningful, noticeable changes... right now! we must take action instead of waiting for the life we want to magically appear.

in a way, this is also a re-evolution... it's an opportunity to roll-back or do-over whatever life has been like until now. once you know that you want something more out of life, there is no going back! you get to create a new vision for your life... a new vision of what is possible.

the revolution is also about the journey we are on - which i believe is not linear and sequential, but instead i see it as a spiral - going around and around like the revolution of a wheel, taking us closer to who we are meant to be in the world. (and there will be much more on this spiral journey later in the book!)

it's about coming full circle... back to YOU.

this is not about *what* you do, it's about who you *are*. it's not about *doing* more, it's about doing *you*... *being* YOU.

when we see the word revolution we think: uprising. rebellion. acts of resistance and defiance. opposing and overthrowing the current regime.

and while this revolution may not have an evil dictator to overthrow, we certainly do have an internal reistance to overcome... that voice in our head that says: *hey, it's better to just stay small, safe, and quiet. this is fine. this life is ok. whatever you do, don't rock the boat.*

that is what this revolution is about... overthrowing that safe, smallness that holds us back from owning our light.

we can choose now to stop trudging through life, going through the motions, feeling a bit dissatisfied, or even a bit lost.

we can choose to do things differently.

we can choose to build a lighthouse. on purpose. so that we may shine our light... the light we were actually born to shine.

how we choose to shine is completely up to each of us.

some of us will do what i did - build a business which is the vehicle by which we shine our light.

some will do it through our careers or work.

some will do it through volunteering and charity work.

some will shine our light by building relationships.

some will do it through our homes and our communities.

others will do it with hobbies and interests and talents.

some will do it simply by being our true selves.

the lighthouse can teach all of us, no matter how we choose to shine.

now, you might be thinking: *"i don't want to change the world, i just want to be happy again!"*

and this is the beautiful thing about shining your light.

when you shine your light, even yes, simply by being happy, you allow and inspire others to do the same. this creates ripples of light that can indeed change the world.

just imagine that for a second.

a whole sea of lighthouses lighting up the world, one small spark of light at a time!

each one of us that stands up and stands tall and shines our light will change humanity.

your light will ignite others.

and so i thank you for being here, for joining me on this journey, for building your lighthouse along with me.

because while it is indeed an internal revolution that takes place, i also think it can be (and i hope it will be) bigger than that... much bigger than me or you or any one person reading this book.

a love story

i've spent the past two years exploring what it would mean to build a lighthouse with my business and my life; studying what we can learn from each component of the lighthouse: the light, the beacon, the tower, the foundation, the spiral staircase, and the harbour; as well as testing strategies that will help us to build each of those components.

and though this is how my *brain* works - working out the pieces of the puzzle, making sense of the lessons and the strategies - this book is actually a story that comes from my *heart and soul*.

i nearly didn't write this book... i was filled with all sorts of doubt.

who am i to write an inspirational, transformational, self-help type of book?

what if it is not inspirational enough? or practical enough?

maybe i should learn more, study more, research more... basically become more 'enough' in some way?

every time i sat down to start writing, or at least outline the chapters and themes, or even do some general brainstorming... i just couldn't do it.

and then one sunny saturday i decided to sit down and read elizabeth gilbert's *big magic*[2], which was gifted to me by a friend, and is a wonderful book all about giving yourself permission to explore your creativity.

there is a phrase that says, "books fall off the shelf," referring to those things that come into your path just when you need them - well this book definitely fell into my hands for a reason, just when i needed it. there are no coincidences!

in the book elizabeth says two things that helped me immensely. the first:

"you are telling the story in a way that's never been told before."

yes! of course, yes. can you imagine if all of the writers and teachers and photographers and artists and hand-makers and designers and musicians and speakers stopped telling their stories because of those nonsense 'who am i?' thoughts? it would be tragic.

and the other thing that struck me:

"please don't write your book to help me. write your book for you. because it's healing for you, or fascinating for you, or because it makes you happy or whatever. write it for you."

i've written lots of books as part of my business but every other book i have written has been a book to help others - they were specifically written as workbooks to teach. i couldn't write this book that way because it just felt different, and now i understand why.

i needed to write it for me, because it brought me joy to do so.

and that changed everything. i could never make this book perfect enough to help everyone. i could never learn enough to help everyone. but i can help me. and the lighthouse really has helped me in profound ways... i wanted to honour those lessons by sharing them here.

i wanted to honour this journey, one that i know so many of us are on... one where we find our purpose in life, forge our path, build a life that we love, and shine our light in some way.

and so i wrote this book as a love story. not as a self-help book or a guide or a handbook. instead it is the story of someone who is simply trying to find their way back to who they are meant to be in the world... back to their heart and soul.

i read somewhere that we should write the story that we ourselves need to hear.

the stories i have needed and valued the most in my journey are the ones that are both inspirational and practical, ones that both touch the soul and ignite the mind, ones that offer both hope and concrete ideas.

the lighthouse story has become that for me. i hope that it can be that for you too.

ignite your light.

be you... authentically you.

learn you.

explore your purpose.

know your why.

define your dream.

seek clarity.

see your light.

part 1

ignite your light

the first, and i imagine the most obvious, component of the lighthouse is the light.

this is the component that first inspired me on my quest... the quest to find my spark again and to do the work that fires me up! and it is the component that i always encourage others to consider first.

you must get back to your light... because it all starts and ends with your light.

what is the light?

it is energy. it is the energy of love, joy, peace, authenticity, inspiration, and growth. this is the stuff that you are here to do in the world... this is your purpose.

your light is you.

the way to ignite your light is simply to BE you.

some of us may first need to find ourselves again. some of us will need to remember who we were before life started to get in the way. some of us will need to give ourselves permission to be the person we feel we are inside. some of us will need to spend some time getting to know our selves again. some of us will need to learn to see ourselves clearly... to see the light that is inside.

but when we do - when we can tap into our own souls, with authenticity and clarity - that is when we will begin to feel lit up from within, once again, as we were born to.

be you

when i first came across the lighthouse quote and began to think about what it would mean to shine i spent a lot of time getting to know *me* again, to *learn* me again.

i was doing some brainstorming one day and i put the phrase 'i am...' in the middle of a blank page and just wrote down all of the things that came to mind. and as i did, i had a memory come to mind, crystal clear as though it were a movie playing in front of my eyes.

right after i had first started my business blog i went home for a visit to canada, and while i was there my bestie's dad was asking about the blog. i found myself stumbling over my words trying to come up with a way to describe what the blog was all about and why i was doing it.

i was so awkward and unsure as i tried to explain my blog: "well you see, i sort of just felt like sharing some of the stuff i was learning about business, you know? like maybe it might help someone, i guess?"

bestie's dad interrupted my rambling and said, "of course you are doing that. you are a teacher. you were born to learn and to teach others. that's what you do. that's who you are."

at the time, when he said that to me i immediately felt better about the blog. i no longer felt like i had to justify this new blog to anyone, and i had the courage to keep going with it.

but that statement didn't really hit me in a profound way until two years later, when i was trying to find my spark again.

that memory came back to me clear as a bell, practically out of the blue. in that moment my entire body went goosebumpy...

i am a teacher.

i hadn't been a 'teacher' (in the career sense) for eight years. i had gone on to be a mother and then a photographer and a designer and a blogger. and over the years i had forgotten what had started me on my journey in the first place - my love of teaching!

remembering this big part of *me* made a piece of the puzzle click into place - my spark felt ignited once again. my blog and my business had a new purpose... teaching! i felt lit up from within... just like a lighthouse.

a year ago i reread a book that i had first read 20 years earlier, when i was young and trying to figure out the meaning of life. *the alchemist* by paulo coehlo[3] called to me, as it sat on my shelf, and i finally picked it up again. it reminded me that i am on a journey to fulfil my purpose.

shortly after that, three separate people at separate times described me as an alchemist, because of the way i help people find the magic in what they do, the way i help them put the pieces of their puzzle together, the way that i can create a spark for someone. it was another powerful moment...

i am an alchemist.

that helped me to see what i do as even more powerful than teaching. it's transformational.

and it gave me something to live up to, something to honour... a purpose bigger than i could have dreamed for myself.

i've also always seen myself as a leader.

all through school and work i was told this about myself... and it has definitely shaped who i am to think of myself in this way. however, i thought my leading days were done as i no longer have a staff or a team or an organization to lead. imagine my surprise to discover that i am still a leader!

i can see now that being a leader really means you are just one step ahead on the journey... hearing the call and taking a leap of faith so that others may too. leading, not by telling others what to do, but by shining a light on the path ahead so that each person on the journey may forge their way and be the hero of their own story.

i am a leader.

recently i was told that i am a healer.

i was a bit shocked actually. this is something i never even imagined about myself. in fact i didn't even know what to say about that... what is a healer? how can i possibly be a healer, i am a teacher! right? i already have my 'thing!'

but what i have come to understand is that healing is simply about shifting energy... getting back to your heart and returning to love. it's remembering who you are in the world... remembering your soul or inner light... being seen or witnessed as the brightest, highest version of yourself.

and hey... that's what the whole lighthouse revolution is all about!

perhaps *i am a healer*. i will keep exploring that one and see where it takes me!

and i have to tell you, when someone sees something in you that you never even imagined for yourself... when someone sees you as something more than you ever believed you could be... well that is a very powerful moment, a profound moment.

the truth is, we don't always see ourselves clearly, and our vision is shaped by our experiences and our circumstances. that is why it is so important to open up and share this journey with others... when we can connect to others, and truly be seen, that is often when we get the most clarity.

and so i've decided something about the light in my lighthouse. i do not wish to visualize that light as a single naked light bulb. instead, my light is a beautiful chandelier, with many individual crystal facets.

i am a teacher. i am a writer. i am a creative. i am strong. i am emotional. i am both introverted and extroverted. i am both intuitive and strategic. i am a healer. i am a leader. i am a rebel. i am an explorer. i am an alchemist. i am a storyteller.

i can be more than one thing. i can be lots of things. i can be many things all at once, even if it seems contradictory.

i can choose to *not* be something any more, if it no longer serves me... i can simply take that little crystal off my chandelier and throw it out the window!

i can also decide to be something new. i can choose who i want to be. i can act as if i already am.

i decide. i am me.

be very aware of how you complete any sentence that starts with "i am..." because this is one of the most powerful phrases in the world... it determines how you see yourself and how the world sees you as well.

what you are insisting on is where your energy will go. it might be time to shift things a little, replace what you've been insisting you are with something new... something that serves you better.

don't just ask: who do *i* think i am? but also ask: who does my soul think i am? who does my money think i am? who does my partner/child/friend think i am? who does my business/career think i am?

these can be powerful questions to ask yourself!

who are you?

and if you aren't too sure right now, just know that you are not alone.

this journey we are on is a winding one! and that sometimes can take us away from who we are or who we wish to be.

but it also takes us back again, back to our light.

this journey you are on is about being you.

your light shines when you be you.

learn you

i am a total sucker for those quizzes that you come across online. archetypes, strengths tests, values tests, personality traits... you name it, i try it. with every little thing i learn about me i feel like i find another little piece of the puzzle.

like any good, challenging puzzle you would never sit down and do it all at once. instead, every time you wander past you add another piece or two... eventually the picture becomes clearer.

sometimes it is a confirmation of something i knew (and maybe just forgot for a while) sometimes it is more of an "ohhhh, that all makes so much sense now!! duh!!"

those types of quizzes can also point to what is not natural for you, or part of your 'make up' so to speak. so you can stop trying to fit your square peg into someone else's round hole! which is so liberating.

recently i did a quiz which gave me a result that actually made me laugh out loud... because it should not have been a surprise at all, yet i was surprised!

i am a rebel.

(anyone who knows me would not find this information shocking at all.)

i've always identified as a rule breaker... the badass that doesn't use capitals.

but as i did this quiz i realized why some of the stuff that has me stuck has me stuck.

i just cannot stand to do things because everyone else is doing them or because there is some sort of expectation on me.

for instance, in the online business space it is very common for coaches and teachers and service providers to do webinars (which are essentially an online presentation where people can follow live or watch a recording). i just cannot bring myself to do a 'webinar.' i have to call it a free live class, or a workshop, or a session, or something else. just calling it *anything* else helps my rebel brain.

when i created my first website everybody told me, "you have to use wordpress. it is THE BEST. it's what everyone uses!" you guessed it, i could not use wordpress. to this day i cannot.

as i have been working on finding myself again and finding my purpose and finding my light, many people have told me: oh you should meditate. you've got to meditate. everyone should meditate. blah blah blah. and that may indeed be so, but i just cannot do it when someone tells me, "oh you've got to."

who the fuck says i've *got* to! you are not the boss of me. i decide what i've got to do!

(can you picture me as a rebellious teenager stomping off and slamming my door after that tirade?)

the way i have found my way to meditation, to exercise, to self-care, to writing, to creating, to teaching... to everything in my life that lights me up... is by flipping it on its head and doing it my way.

doing it the rebel way.

44 3333 33

at first - even though this book was tapping me on the shoulder and i knew i really wanted to write it - i was still feeling totally stuck because i had this idea in my head that it was going to be so bland and boring. (because i had the idea that non-fiction books are almost always bland and boring). i also felt constrained by the 'proper grammar' thing: capitals, proper paragraphs, no ellipses, etc... as well as the idea that i had to plan out my chapters and headings and who knows what other rules i had to follow.

when i did that quiz it reminded me about me.

i realized i needed to write the rebel version of a book.

(and this book seems hardly rebellious now that i am a few thousand words in, but just making the decision to do it my way was enough to get me started!)

if i can tap into what feels rebellious about what i am doing i can actually get myself unstuck quite often. i often realize i was not even really stuck at all; i was just coming at it from the wrong direction.

if i feel like i am breaking some rules and doing it my way, i am good to go. if i feel like i am conforming, or caving to expectations, or being told i "have to" - i just automatically get in my own way.

it's powerful to understand this about myself, because i can work with that... knowing that means i can reframe my thinking on some things; i can find the rebel version and keep going!

if i can focus on *why* i am doing something (instead of what i'm expected to do)... if i can focus on *how* it will allow me to be true to me... and if i can do it in a way that sets me apart from what others do... then i can move forward.

one of the most important things you can do is *learn you* - and this is why! every little puzzle piece helps!

there is one thing that i want you to remember though; *learning you* does not mean *fixing you*. you are not broken! you do not need to be fixed or changed or corrected. you are simply you... and this is simply about *being* you.

learn you. learn what lights you up. learn what makes your soul shine.

future you

when i was in my early 20s and contemplating the meaning of life - my mom gave me a book of poems that included the poem *warning* by jenny joseph.[4] it begins...

"*when i am an old woman i shall wear purple with a red hat...*"

do you remember it?

it pops into my head every now and then, especially when i am with women who say something like:

"one day i would love to be like/dress like/act like that woman over there"

or

"oh wow, that is exactly what i aspire to be one day!"

or

"someday i am totally going to do/try that..."

when i hear comments like that (or catch myself making them!) there is always one question that comes to mind...

what are you waiting for?

is there a magic date when it will be ok to 'wear purple?'

is there a certain time when it will be the right time to start being that person you are longing to be?

maybe we ought to start practicing right now.

as you are building your lighthouse, imagine standing across the harbour and seeing yourself as that old woman on the other side - seeing 'future you' - visualizing yourself in the role that you are longing to play (your version of wearing purple!)

i think sometimes we feel stuck because we have a foot on both sides of the gulf - part of us is staying in the 'now' space (which is safe and easy and known... even if it doesn't really light us up!) and the other part has crossed the harbour and is building something that will allow us to be that future, ignited self.

we go from being confident to unsure and back again. we go from dreaming big to being scared and backing off again. we go from feeling totally on fire and on purpose and lit up from within to feeling overcome by the darkness with the waves crashing in.

it's hard.

i try to visualize that future me on the other side of the harbour as often as possible - to see that future as a reality and to trust that it's simply there just waiting for me.

and i try to embody that future me right now as often as possible... to act as if...

if she is an author, i will call myself that now. if she meditates and walks by the sea and does yoga in the sand, i can start doing that now. if she is a world class speaker and leader and teacher, i can practice those things right now. if she wears whatever the fuck she likes and swears and has tattoos and loves intentional jewellery and funky nails... yep, i can start right now.

and if she morphs into something a little different over time, no problem!

we are here to change and evolve... when i am an old woman i will be whatever i will be.

but it is a lot more productive to dream and live 'as if' right now, than it is just sitting back and waiting for the perfect day to come along.

start now.

be weird

when i first started the *build a little biz* blog i tried to be professional and write properly, following all the grammar and punctuation and sentence rules. and the whole time i would write it just didn't feel right... i didn't feel like *me*.

even from the time that i was first teaching i never used capitals in my personal emails and messages. i remember a long time ago, one of my friends saying she always knew a message came from me, even without looking at the sender... she said: "who do you think you are? e. e. cummings?"

so when i was trying to be all professional and proper with my writing, i would read it back to myself and it would feel like something someone else had written. i was really struggling to get the blog going... i felt like i had writers block all of the time, even though in my head i felt like i had so much to say!

after fighting my way through my first couple of blog posts i thought: what am i doing? no one else is probably ever even going to read this blog, besides my mom... and she loves me no matter what! i am just going to do it my way.

and in that moment i gave myself permission to simply be *me*.

to write like i talk. to never use capitals. to swear if i want to. to use as many sentence fragments and ellipses as i feel like using.

and that permission turned out to be one the best things i ever could have done, for myself and my business.

not only could i finally write - the writer's block was gone and the floodgates were open - but my lack of capitalization became a distinct and important part of my brand.

to my surprise people did indeed read my blog and it grew to be quite popular. my message has always been, even then, that you need to be 100% you. and when i gave myself permission to be me (and the world did not fall apart!) that in turn gave permission to my readers to do the same.

not only that, but my style of writing and imagery stands out. i have had people copy my words and my images over the years and my readers have called them on it - knowing that the work was actually mine, just because of the lack of capitals and the way i write.

another benefit of being a 'badass rebel rule-breaker who never uses capitals' is that the people who don't like it keep moving on. they don't stick around! the people who like it go on to buy my workbooks or join my workshops or work with me personally. it has been a great polarizer... separating my most awesome people from the ones who are not in the right place for either of us.

right now, do you feel like you can be 100% you in all areas of work and life?

or do you feel like you need to hide parts of you, gloss over parts of you, down play parts of you, or change parts of you in some way.

perhaps you worry that some things are too 'out there' or too weird or some people wouldn't get it or it would turn some people off or you just don't want to try to explain.

or maybe you are just simply trying to be professional, polished, logical, strategic, safe, smart, plain, quiet, proper (or whatever other quality it feels like we *ought* to be.)

i encourage you to let more of *you* shine through.

what makes you weird? what about you is quirky? what is unusual about the way you do things? what do you keep hidden from most people? what do you 'quiet' or dim in order to play it safe? what would surprise people, if they only knew? what feels just a bit too scary to share?

it's time to let you shine through.

because how can you shine your light if you are hiding you? stop hiding.

there is nothing more liberating than deciding to share your weirdness with the world, deciding to break whatever rules there are about who it is you are supposed to be, and giving yourself permission to just be 100% you.

weird is good. it makes you memorable. it allows you to feel authentic and real. it allows others to really know you and connect with you. it polarizes.

so let your weird light shine bright!

the stuff that makes you different helps you to make a difference.

your purpose

many years ago i started having some very weird dreams. i call them dreams but really they are something in between waking and sleeping, more of an intense dreamy state than an actual vivid dream.

when i have one of these dreams i wake up feeling like i have lost something.

when they first started, the dream was that i had lost my wedding rings: i would even wake up some-times searching my closet shelf for my rings, which of course were right there where i left them.

other times i wake up feeling like i have forgotten something.

sometimes it is a living thing, like a pet or a baby, that i have forgotten to care for or feed, and now it is dying due to my neglect... sometimes i have forgotten to do some important paperwork or take some sort of pill, or complete some other task that was absolutely essential. the forgotten thing always seems to be buried deep on a bottom shelf in my closet.

so the dreams have taken different shapes over the years but i always wake with an intense sensation that i have lost something or forgotten something that is very important. i always wake up feeling very unsettled, like clarity is always just out of reach.

a few months ago i had the opportunity to get some wonderful insight into these dreams.

one of my friends is highly intuitive - you might think of her as a medium or a psychic... she is able to communicate with her soul guides, in fact they will even come through and talk to us directly.

after she was brave enough to share her gifts with me and we had become close, i had this niggling feeling - like a tap tap tap on my shoulder - that i should ask her about my dreams, and so i did.

this is exactly what her guides said to me (apparently they had just been waiting for me to ask!):

> this is the amygdala part of your brain triggering off a series of flashing 'omg i forgot this!' moments - getting your attention just

before or during sleep when there is room for the message to get through.

this is about forgetting to be you. forgetting who you were born to be. forgetting that you are worthy of love, connection, and success.

this is a message from your soul but triggered by your amygdala (the fight or flight part of your brain.)

your role, if you choose to accept it (the guides are quite cheeky!) is to remember who you were born to be - not the person you *think* you need to be in order to be loved, worthy, successful, spiritual.

this doesn't mean that you need to leave behind who you are now or how you walk through the world... what it means is coming back to who you were and had decided to be before you arrived, this time before and just after birth when the purest and most clear intentions are made for your journey here.

think of these dreams as your alarm clock going off regularly to remind you to listen to your soul and go with your heart... to hear the call, to surrender to the energy, and to go wherever it is taking you.

whether you are into the whole notion of psychic intuition and soul guides or not, i think the message here is still so important.

do you remember who you were born to be? or what you were born to do? before the world told you who and what and how you should be?

when i received this message about my dreams, well, it all made sense!

i had lost myself, i had forgotten who i was born to be, i had forgotten to take care of something very important, something that was neglected and hidden away...

myself. my soul. my inner spark.

and so my quest became finding my purpose... my soul's true purpose.

i have indeed learnt many practical strategies and tools for honing in on my purpose, getting clarity on the work i am here to do, igniting my spark.

but - and i know this will sound cliché - what i discovered is that your purpose is not actually a destination... your purpose is in fact, the journey.

your purpose here is to seek your purpose. your purpose is to be fully you. your purpose is to follow what is calling out to you or whispering quietly in your ear. your purpose is to do things with joy and to give and receive love and to learn and to grow and to evolve and to overcome.

your purpose is to find what lights you up because you are here to shine your light.

your road so far

i think that reflection is one of the most important things we can do on this journey - to take a look back at 'the road so far.'

how do you know where you are going if you don't know where you've been or how far you've come!

when you look back at your road so far, your passions are signposts that point to your calling. your passions were never meant to be long term, sustainable things, rather they arise to take you further on your journey to your purpose. look back at your journey and see where your passions have led you, what ties them together.

look also for the big ah ha moments, the little nudges, the signs or messages, the 'sliding doors' moments or turning points, the people and situations that changed the course of your life - they can all help you get a picture of who you are and what you are here to do.

another thing to look for in the road so far are the times where you felt like you lived in the shadow -

maybe you didn't feel ignited at all, maybe life or work felt a little dreary, maybe you weren't even close to living your purpose - but you still found little pockets of light.

for instance, i can look back to teaching math and science and remember not feeling particularly excited about the subject matter - but what i did love was coming up with clever ways to teach a big idea, ways to make the concepts click. i felt ignited when students said: oh wow, now i get it! thank you!

i can look back to when i was teaching specific marketing strategies to biz builders and didn't really have my mojo for that work, but i really loved those little moments when i could encourage someone to tap into their purpose, their authenticity and light, and really get their message out in a big way.

when i had my photography business i loved that i could explore and express my creativity. i know now that photography was a passion (never meant to be a long term thing) and it definitely pointed me on a road to my purpose. the little pocket of light occurred for me when i shared an image (combining photographs with quotes or lyrics) that would move people deeply. i loved when i made people cry... i felt like my work was powerful and evocative and transformational.

those three things are all part of my purpose... and part of the work i am doing now with the lighthouse revolution!

as i've already said, take some time to learn you. your strengths, personality traits, archetypes, beliefs, values, desires... the stuff that lights you up, the stuff you would do even if you didn't get paid for it, the stuff that you would fight for, fiercely.

the signposts on your journey, the things that light you up, the things that make you *you* are all simply pieces of a puzzle. the more pieces you find and fit, the more the picture becomes clear. and like most challenging jigsaw puzzles... this can't be done in one sitting. remember that it is actually the journey of finding the pieces that matters, not the final picture.

one more thing you can do is PLAY! you find your purpose by *doing*, not waiting. so play, have fun, follow joy, explore, evolve, learn, try, grow... take the steps that feel light. your life's purpose is what you say it is. this isn't meant to be a chore or a task. there are no rules here... no final destination.

your purpose is simply where your heart is. it's how you choose to live your life and shine your light.

your why

related to your purpose is your why.

sometimes these words are used interchangeably, and you should absolutely look at these ideas in a way that makes sense to you and your journey.

i think of your purpose as WHO you are meant to be and WHAT you are meant to do. your WHY is the reason you are doing it... the motivation that drives you.

simon sinek - in his book *start with why*[5] and his ted talk *why great leaders inspire action*[6] - says: *"people don't buy what you do; they buy why you do it."*

this is a really powerful idea and one that i think will make a difference to any one of us as we do the work we need to do to build our lighthouse and live a life that lights us up.

you yourself won't buy into *what* you do, until you buy *why* you are doing it. you need to know your why for everything that you do.

knowing your why is a great way to ignite your light. your why can be a powerful force that drives what you do. it pulls you and draws you in - like moths to a flame - instead of feeling like you are pushing all of the time.

when i was first starting out in business, my photography biz was very part time. my why - the thing that was really driving me - was to have a bit of spending money. at that time, we had just moved to australia and we were borrowing money to move there and live there and study there, and i hated the fact that i felt like i had to justify every dollar spent. i just wanted my own money to buy new shoes or a new handbag! i was fiercely independent and i had been making my own money since i started babysitting at 13 years old, so that was a powerful why for me at the time.

over time my why evolved - and my business also evolved - i started helping other women in biz and my why was about achieving fulfilment, freedom, and flexibility in my life.

more recently, when i understood the meaning of my crazy dreams, my why became about exploring my soul's purpose. my choices and actions were driven by that why - and my biz evolved once again. my biz is a reflection of me, of my soul and my journey, it is a way to find and fulfil and share my purpose.

i realized that my purpose was to help others find their purpose (their light) and share it with the world. my BIG why - the core belief that drives what i do - is that i truly believe each of is us here for a reason; we are here to shine our light. and nothing makes me more sad than to see people whose light has been dimmed, supressed, ignored, or extinguished. so that is my big why.

what is your why?

it is very helpful to have personal whys that drive each of the things that you do: your goals, projects, dreams, and creative pursuits.

be connected to WHAT you want by being connected to WHY you want it.

my money why was once having some 'shoe money' of my own. now my money why is that i don't ever, ever want to go back to a 'job' - this is just not an option! believe me, this why keeps me very motivated to do the work i need to do to earn money from my business

your personal whys for each of your goals can be a powerful force to help you do the work you need to do to achieve what you want.

but also be sure you know your BIG why.

this is the core value, belief, or desire at the heart of what you do - the purpose you are feeling called towards. other things might change - what you do and how you do it and where you are going next all might evolve - but your why is the thing that is driving you at the core.

to get to the heart of your BIG why, dive deeper. ask why and then keep asking why.

i call it the toddler test. have you ever had a toddler ask you why? you know they don't stop! so sit with someone and try to explain to them why you do what you do - you can start with your own personal why if you'd like - and get them to play the role of the toddler - to keep asking: "but why? i know, but why? ok then, but why?" use this to dig deeper and deeper until you get past the whats and the hows of what you do - to get to the core of it all... the why.

also, go back to your journey - your road so far and your signposts - those can be clues to your why as well. how has your why evolved from when you first started your journey to where you are now?

sometimes your big why can be a hard thing to pinpoint, or to put into words. remember - this is a journey. the more you talk about it, the more the words will come. the more you explore and follow your heart, the more clarity you will find. and even if you can't put it into words, tapping into how your why *feels* is still a very powerful force!

your spark

when i first started to explore what it would mean to shine my light like a lighthouse, i was trying to find my mojo again.

in the midst of having babies and raising kids and working at home and building my business and blogging about business... i lost my way. i lost myself. i lost what had gotten me started on this journey in the first place.

my light was not shining bright at all. in fact it was pretty dim and kind of flickering... like a sad old string of christmas lights!

in my quest to learn *me* again, and to figure out who karen was NOW, i rediscovered some of what i had lost.

somehow, in the effort to build my business, i lost what made it special to me in the first place. i lost my creative spark. i lost sight of the stuff i really loved doing in an effort to sell what i thought people wanted me to do. i was trying to be everything to everyone, all of the time.

i wasn't really tapping into what makes me ME.

and i wasn't adding any fuel to the tank. how can your light shine brightly without any fuel?

i realized that to be my best i needed to be doing what lights me up. i needed to make space for my own kind of creativity again (not to serve anyone else but simply to keep my spark ignited.) i needed to make time to learn and explore... writing and journaling and being curious about the world around me. and i needed to create opportunities to teach and connect with others, sharing ideas and inspiration.

without time and space for these things in my life i do not have enough fuel to keep my light shining bright.

we also need to take care of ourselves first... to take good care of our own light. exercise, healthy food, rest, relaxation, pampering, meditation, laughter, fun... these are all as important to our souls as they are to our bodies... self-care is really all about you being your own lighthouse keeper. and the best thing is that you get to do it your way!

sometimes people will ask me: "i have so many things i am into and that i love and that i'm pas-sionate about... how do i pick just one thing to be my lighthouse?"

the answer is: you don't!

all of the things that you love and that light you up do not have to become your life's work. they do not have to be your mission or your purpose.

they can simply be what make you YOU.

they can help you to shine bright by being the fuel that lights you up, giving you the energy and the passion and motivation to go out and do what you long to do.

each of the things you need and love in your life can act as a light switch... why not have lots of light switches?

what lights you up? what fuels your spark? how can you take care of you first?

your BIG vision

when i first thought about the lighthouse as a symbol for the business and life i was building, the symbol was just for me.

i carried on building my business, i carried on learning and exploring and growing, and that was fine. i was playing it fairly small, and fairly safe, doing all of the things i was supposed to do, and plodding along quite nicely. it was all okay. fine.

and then one day the seed of an idea was planted... to share the lighthouse with others in a much broader and bolder way.

and suddenly, what was once satisfactory was now simply not enough. it felt uncomfortable. it felt like something was missing. it felt like perhaps there could be something more out there, just beyond my reach, if only i could just get a little bit closer.

i began to think bigger. i began to dream bigger. i began to plan bigger.

and it was scary as hell.

of course it was. your ego wants you to stay safe and small and comfy and FINE. so dreaming bigger really triggers some big fear and some big 'i am not enough' thoughts.

but do you know what else happens when you think bigger?

things flow. things shift. things start to fall into place, beyond what you could ever have hoped for.

it's a bit like placing an order with the universe. if we are thinking: *oh, i will just have the small safe FINE thing*, then that is what will be delivered.

but if we think: *you know what? i think i will have the BIG thing. the MOST AWESOME thing possible.*

well the universe wants to deliver that thing to you just the same.

when i began to think of the lighthouse as something bigger than a little talisman just for me, when i began to think of it as something that could help others, when i began to think of it as a *revolution*... some awesome things began to happen.

my first post about the lighthouse became the most popular post i had ever written. people began to tell me what the lighthouse meant to them. people began to send me lighthouses! the components of the lighthouse and what we could learn from each of them began to take shape. teachers and strategies and resources fell into my lap. opportunities to speak and to teach began to open up.

if i hadn't decided to go bigger with my lighthouse, i don't think any of that would have happened. it would have stayed as a little symbol just for me, as i plodded along my path, never uncomfortable but never really remarkable either.

as we explore what ignites our light it is so important to think a little bit bigger, to think beyond the horizon of what feels safe and fine and doable and within reach.

think BIG.

what would you do if you were not afraid?

what would you do if you couldn't fail? if money were no object? if no one would think you were a weirdo or a loser or completely off your rocker?

what would it look like? what would it feel like? what would you be thinking about and talking about? how would you be spending your time? who would you be?

imagine it as though it is reality... as though it has already happened.

creating a BIG vision for yourself, for your life, for your work or your biz, for your plans or your goals... can be a wonderful way to ignite your light.

i will often sit down and just do some big dreaming - grab a blank piece of paper and some colourful pens, or maybe go off and create a big vision pin-board on pinterest, or simply just close my eyes and dream.

especially if i am feeling like my spark is burning a little low, or i am feeling a bit stuck in some way, i will often realize that i haven't thought about my BIG vision in a while and i can see that i am back to playing it pretty small and safe.

having a big vision for yourself is about claiming your dream... it's about deciding to be the highest, brightest version of yourself, deciding to have the best version of a life for yourself. and who doesn't want that?!

don't compare your big vision to anyone else's. in fact people rarely share their big vision so there is no sense in comparing your journey to anyone else's! there are too many pieces of the puzzle to make a fair comparison. what is big to you might feel safe to someone else, and vice versa!

plus, what feels BIG right now to you might soon enough feel small and safe again, because we grow and evolve and so must our vision. we must revisit our vision often... keep seeking clarity, keep pushing the boundaries out a little bigger.

think of your big vision: do you tingle with possibility, with excitement, and yes with a little bit of fear? if not... your vision might not be big enough!

dream BIG dreams.

your role

the thing about dreaming big dreams, the thing that no one warns you about, is that it triggers these crazy fears and thoughts in our minds.

this is normal.

there is also something else that no one tells you about... we ALL have crazy fears and thoughts going through our minds (even those people who already shine so bright!)

who am i to shine my light?

who am i to be boldly, bravely 100% me?

who am i to have big dreams and a big vision about the life i want to live?

i am not enough.

i don't know enough.

i haven't done enough.

i am not special.

(i think you get the idea.)

not only have i learnt that these thoughts are NORMAL - everyone has them - i've also learnt where they come from.

they are from the ego, trying desperately to keep us small and safe and comfy and fine.

and so, knowing that, when those thoughts start arriving in your head you need to whisper back:

"who am i NOT to?"

because really, who ARE you not to?

you are here for a reason. you are here to shine your light... to live your purpose, to BE YOU. and who are you NOT to do that? who are any of us NOT to do that?

i can remember when i was first starting to teach as part of my business - i was writing workbooks and creating workshops helping women in business with their marketing and branding.

there was always this niggling thought in the back of my head...

"who am i to teach this stuff? i don't have a business degree. i am not a marketing expert. i am just a teacher."

and one day i had a moment when that exact thought was running through my head and i could suddenly, clearly see what i had been telling myself. i actually laughed out loud and thought: *listen to yourself. you have just said...*

"who am i to teach this stuff... i am just a teacher."

seriously?

i was a trained, qualified teacher with my own personal experience in marketing and branding a successful business, and i had studied the craft obsessively. i knew i was good at making things click for people with my teaching strategies, and i knew that i consistently helped people be more successful in their own businesses... i knew because they told me!

who was i NOT to embrace my gifts as a teacher? who was i NOT to help others?

just because of my own insecurities? that is just so silly!

that 'not enough' thought of "i am just a teacher" still goes through my head sometimes, but since that moment i try to never let it pass unstopped... i always try to catch it and replace it with:

"yes, i AM a teacher. an awesome one. who am i NOT to teach?"

i think sometimes we get trapped playing a role that we no longer fit. in my case the role was:

stay at home mum. supportive, doctor's wife. school volunteer. very part time photographer. newbie blogger. interested in learning about lots of things. likes helping others. was once a teacher.

owning the fact that i am indeed *still* a teacher shifted things a little.

starting to dream just a little bigger shifted things a lot.

i began to think about the role i actually wanted to play (instead of the role i was currently playing.)

successful business owner. bestselling author. world renown speaker. first class teacher. thought leader. healer. inspirational. worthy. confident. feminine. strong. badass.

i think maybe we ought to start saying no to the roles that feel like they box us in, or feel like they no longer fit, or just don't light us up any more.

and start thinking about the role we would like to play, to be the leading star of our own lives.

who do you want to be?

who would you be if that BIG vision of yours was a reality?

perhaps it is time to start learning that role... practicing for it.

to act as if.

igniting your light is about being you, learning you, and believing in future you. it's about exploring your purpose and knowing your why and having clarity on your big vision. it's about knowing what fuels your light so that you can keep shining.

be a beacon.

share you.

beam your light outwards.

be visible.

speak your truth.

tell your stories.

connect with your boats.

own your light.

part 2

be a beacon

the next component of the lighthouse is the beacon.

think about the beacon of a lighthouse: it is a signal, a beam, a message... a guiding light for the boats at sea.

when you shine your light, that is what your light becomes to others... a beacon.

your light is not meant to be hidden inside: dimmed, diminished, or contained; you are not meant to shine quietly or discretely or in isolation.

(if the lighthouse brings to mind a feeling of isolation it is only because you are forgetting about all of the boats the lighthouse touches with its light every day!)

you are here to connect with others, to communicate, to share yourself, and your stories, and the light that lives inside.

being a beacon is about being visible. it's about raising your voice... being seen and being heard. it's about owing your truth... saying: hey world, this is me.

not only are you here to BE you, you are here to SHARE you.

your story

the lighthouse is meant to remind you that you are here to ignite your light and you are meant to beam your light out to others.

but i know that many people feel like they haven't got a light to shine... anything special to share, anything unique to offer. perhaps they haven't found their purpose or are not feeling very ignited about anything. maybe they feel like the world doesn't really need their light, that it doesn't really matter or make a difference, or that someone else is already doing it better.

i know this feeling well; i have struggled with these exact thoughts myself.

and there is one simple thing that has helped me in ways i couldn't even imagine. it's made the biggest difference to my journey, and it's something that i want to encourage you to try.

tell your stories.

telling my stories truly has made the biggest difference in my journey.

back when i had a business blog, i used to write a lot about strategies that helped me to build a business, and i always made an effort to be authentic: to be myself, to write like i talk, and to share my own stories. my goal was to share practical information and to make it click for women in biz, and i always found that sharing stories and examples helped with that.

but my biggest lesson in story telling came not when i was sharing helpful practical information, but when instead i decided to be very vulnerable and share the honest truth about how hard i often found it to build my business.

before i started the lighthouse revolution, i had been blogging about business for a number of years. one new year i decided to write a series on my 'biz resolutions' - and those resolutions, at the core, were raw stories about: comparing myself to others; getting sucked into negativity; worrying about what others think, do and say; being hard on myself... all of the traps that so many of us fall into.

my goal with that series was simply to 'keep it real' - to pull back the curtains, so to speak, and shine a light on the struggles that so many of us face, as well as perhaps sharing a bit of inspiration to do things differently in the new year.

those blog posts were, at the time, the most vulnerable pieces i had ever written. i wrote those stories for me - i was tired of this trend where people seemed to always act online as though everything was always awesome, often much better than reality, and that they had no weakness. i wrote those posts because i needed to just be me and be real.

i did hope that someone out there would read my stories and know they were not alone, but i also thought my posts might backfire and people would be pissed they hadn't received practical strategies, or annoyed that i was just going on and on about my own experiences as a woman in biz.

to my surprise, those posts became the most popular posts i had written. the comments and emails and messages flooded in.

when i shared my stories it was really about owning my truth. no more hiding behind this polished, fake curtain. but what happened is that people reading those stories suddenly knew they were not alone. they had one other person out there who would be real with them and would honour their journey too. someone who would not think they were a loser for having all of these struggles!

when i shared my stories i gave others permission to do the same... it was safe to be real and raw and authentic.

it was one of those moments that shaped what i would do from then on with my business - with my writing, with speaking... with any place i was connecting with others - telling real, raw, vulnerable, stories.

when you tell your stories, it frees you. it heals you. it empowers you. you are saying to yourself: my voice does matter. my stories have shaped me and i honour that.

you do not have to let your stories own you... you get to own the story. tell it your way and on your terms. big or small... complex or simple... your stories matter. and even if someone else has told a similar story, you get to tell it in a way that has never been done before.

tell your stories for you.

and remember that talking is not the only way to tell a story - you can share your stories with art, photographs, music, writing, craft, teaching, singing, movement... there are many ways to tell a story and share your 'voice' - use whatever feels like a gateway to your light, to your soul.

there is something very powerful about feeling seen and heard, so even as you share your stories be sure to listen to others tell theirs. when you sit with a friend and talk about your journey, or share something that lights you up, or talk about the kind of person you long to be... be sure to spend as much time listening to her tell you the same.

see the light in others.

each of us is longing to be seen and heard. each of us is on a journey that is not always easy, and doesn't always make sense. we are all doing the best we can with what we have. we all deserve the chance to shine. we all deserve to raise our voice and be visible.

resonate

the next time i noticed how powerful it is to tell your story was when i first started writing about the lighthouse as a symbol to teach us how to shine our light in the world, and first called it 'the lighthouse revolution' on my blog.

i was honestly blown away by the comments i received.

people wrote to tell me how much the lighthouse as a symbol meant to them.

they wrote to describe what stands out to them the most when they think about the lighthouse.

they wrote to tell me their own stories of feeling lost, stuck, or like they were spinning in circles... and how the lighthouse gave them a new hope.

they wrote to say thank you for sharing something so personal to me, for being vulnerable and real.

the message i heard over and over again was: *"wow. that really resonates with me."*

i think that is such a beautiful and powerful word. *resonate.*

resonate can be defined as: to ring true. to vibrate strongly. to strike a chord.

as someone who is building a business, i can say that is really the impact you always hope to have with your communication efforts!

but i think it is true for any aspect of life - when you tell your story and someone else says "wow. me too!" it is very empowering. and it is freeing as well... it's like that vice grip of fear that we have at sharing our story just loosens right up the moment someone says they are so glad you did.

so i began a quest of sorts to explore more about what it means to resonate.

why do some stories or messages resonate strongly, while others just fall flat?

and why do some things resonate for some people, but not at all for others?

and what exactly does one have to do in order to resonate with someone else?

i looked back on my own journey to the lighthouse revolution and tried to pinpoint the things i did that resonated, the stuff that made a difference. and i also looked at the choices i made that completely fell flat as well.

i studied other women and businesses and brands and stories that really seemed to resonate strongly with people.

what i found was not really surprising, but it is still worth repeating.

here is what resonates:

when people allow themselves to be real: to be open and vulnerable and raw and let their true selves shine through.

when people allow themselves to be moved: to show emotion, to get fired up, to be silly or funny or wild or crazy or angry or devastated.

when people allow themselves to get personal: to share their own journeys and what made a difference and what they've learned.

and here's the thing: if you want your story... your work... your light... to resonate with others, it needs to resonate with *you* first.

as i look back on my own journey, the thing that stands out to me the most is that the times where i shared my story in a vulnerable, personal, moving way are the times people told me: "that resonates."

or "wow. that is just what i needed to hear/read/see today."

or "thank you for sharing that. it's so good to know i am not alone."

those times are also the ones where i experienced the biggest shifts in my journey, where i learnt the most, or where the path just opened up for me.

story is the key.

and it's not been just about *sharing* my stories (though that certainly is a powerful way to beam your light... to speak your truth and connect with others too.)

it's also been about simply being open and curious to *explore* my stories.

looking back on my 'road so far' and wondering: what were the turning points and 'ah ha's? who were the people that impacted me most? what lessons have i learned along the way?

it's amazing how we let our stories own us - define us, shape our worlds - when instead we should own our stories.

we should decide when we no longer need to hang on to a story any more, let it define us any longer. we should learn what we can from our stories and then choose to write the next chapter... our way.

telling your story isn't even so much about connecting with other people - helping other people, or letting others know they are not alone.

that stuff is just a really awesome side effect... the icing on the cake.

the real power behind telling your story is how it connects you to *you*.

telling your story is about owning your truth.

and healing your past.

and exploring your journey.

and putting the pieces of your life-puzzle together.

stories resonate - as we have already learned. but the reason they resonate for others is because they resonate for you.

your story matters. *to you.* and so sharing your stories is one of the most powerful things you can do to own your light, and own your truth.

when i was first thinking of writing this book, i was super excited (because i do love to tell stories!) and this particular book has been tap tap tapping me on the shoulder for a long time!

but as i've mentioned, i also found myself rather stuck. i was having trouble creating an outline for a book that would be helpful to others.

the stuckness dissolved when i decided to write the book for me, to honour everything that the lighthouse has taught me and continues to teach me. and because it helps me to keep healing and keep learning and keep growing. and because it really feels like in doing so i am writing the next chapter of my own story - which is so empowering!

if it helps others too - that would be awesome. if it changes the world for just one other person, that would be really freaking cool.

but even if it doesn't resonate with anyone else... that's totally ok. because it's *my* love story. and sharing it is the biggest act of self-love i have ever undertaken.

and because story telling is a powerful way to shine my light.

teach

i believe that one of the best things we can include in our lighthouse is teaching.

teach what you love. teach what lights you up. teach to share your light with others.

for many people, they hear that suggestion and automatically the inner voice in their head comes up with all sorts of reasons why that will never happen...

i am not a teacher.

i am not trained to teach.

i have no certificate. or degree. (or whatever other piece of paper we think we need to have.)

i don't know enough to teach others.

i wouldn't even know where to begin.

there are already other people teaching this stuff.

and yes, you could probably keep making all sorts of excuses and defending all of those excuses. they may all in fact be true.

but it doesn't change this one simple thing, which i believe wholeheartedly:

teaching is one of the most powerful things you can do to change the world.

to change YOUR world.

teaching helps you to ignite your own light. teaching helps you beam your light out to others. teaching helps you find your voice, be visible, and own who you are in the world. teaching is empowering - it builds your sense of confidence and self-worth. teaching allows you to connect with others, to share what you do with others in a way that is authentic and is of service... it creates a connection between people that is like no other.

what can you teach?

anything that you are good at. anything that helps others. anything that people ask you for help with already. anything people tell you they would love to learn from you. anything you are learning yourself. anything you are passionate about. anything that you are curious about.

and this is one of the most powerful things to realize: most of us feel called to teach *something*.

i am going to make a guess that deep down, there is a little whisper inside of you that says: "you know, you could help others with this too." i believe this is very common amongst those of us longing to live our purpose... to live a life that lights us up.

because we feel called to teach the very thing that we need to learn most ourselves.

i felt called to teach what i was learning about the lighthouse because it was what i needed to learn the most too... how to create a life that would allow me to own my light in this world.

the lighthouse revolution is the lesson that i need to learn myself, which was why i feel called to teach it.

what you feel called to teach is what you need to learn too.

and, by the way, you don't have to call it *teaching*.

you can coach, mentor, write, share, assist, help, guide, lead, workshop, talk, riff, blog, explore, investigate, demonstrate, instruct, explain, advise, illustrate, inform, brainstorm, or nurture. or any other word that feels just right to you! you choose.

but the common denominator is this:

you helping one other person (even as you help yourself).

that is all teaching is. sharing your experience (or knowledge, or strengths, or talents, or ideas, or strategies) with someone else.

and the idea that you don't know enough yet, are not far enough on your journey yet, or are not ready yet, to teach... well throw that out the window.

you only need to be one step ahead.

one step.

that's all.

when i was a middle school science teacher i walked into the classroom on my very first day with a degree in science; i had a double major with honours so i certainly felt like i knew my stuff. only to discover when i opened the textbook that, for the most part, i didn't have a clue about the science i was there to teach!

so every night i taught myself the content that i had to teach the next day.

for the first year, and for the first of any new content i have ever had to teach, i was only ever *one step ahead.*

what i did have was a strong desire to make things click for my students. i genuinely wanted to make science fun for them, and i wanted it to feel 'doable' - like it didn't have to be something super hard and scary. i wanted to ignite that little spark in them - the 'wow, this is cool' spark - that little ah ha moment where everything starts to make sense.

that desire has never left me.

so you don't actually need a certificate that says you can teach. you just need to have the desire to help someone else.

you don't *need* a world stage or a fancy online program or a physical classroom somewhere. you *can* have that stuff of course, but you get to decide. you can meet with a group at the local café and talk about something you are all interested in learning. you can start a blog and write about what you are passionate about. you can create videos for youtube. you can hold a session at a library or a community centre. you can make a little worksheet or guide or checklist and share it with people. you can call up a friend and tell her about the very thing you are learning yourself.

the bottom line is that you get to do it your way. you can work to your strengths. you can do what lights you up.

there are no rules.

(and whatever rules you think there are: ask, "WHO SAYS?" and then break them. and then make your own.)

the thing to remember is that teaching is about sharing you. and connecting with others.

and it's about learning too. because when you teach you learn. there is nothing that will accelerate your own learning journey the way teaching will.

when i first started out i taught science to middle school kids. then i taught general business tips to mums who were building a little biz, just like me. then i taught branding and marketing strategies. then i taught visual marketing and graphic design. then i taught mindset and getting unstuck. and now i am teaching about your purpose and your journey.

every little step i have taken, every little door i have opened, every little thing i have learned and then taught to others... it has all led me to where i am right now.

which is exactly where i am meant to be.

but i have no doubt in my mind that my journey is not over.

there is more to learn. and for me, that means there is more to teach.

your mission

one day i read a great article online that was entitled *in praise of women who give all the fucks.*[7]

it got me thinking: what is something i really care about? a thing that i would fight to the limit for? something that would prompt me to unfriend or unfollow people for being dicks? what do i give a huge fuck about?

one issue that gets me really fired up is LGBTQ equality and acceptance.

which, at the core, is the RIGHT to BE YOU. to live your life exactly as YOU. to be and to love whomever you want. without shame. without hiding. to never have your light extinguished because of someone else's definition of, or expectation of, marriage, gender, or sexuality.

there isn't a specific reason why this issue feels like my fight. i do not have a personal story to share. it has nothing to do with my own journey, my business, or my immediate family.

but i do have best friends and family in the LGBTQ community. i have kids who are going to grow up in a world of our making. and i have a heart.

love is love. love is louder. nothing else should really matter. and i just don't get *why* it matters... people just want the right to BE.

this is an issue i give a huge fuck about.

people are actually dying because of shame. because of hate. because of judgement. because they aren't being accepted exactly as they are. because they feel that they cannot live exactly as they are. and that is just simply not ok.

and because i have been so fired up about this, especially recently in light of marriage equality and transgender acceptance, i've spent a bit of time thinking about WHY it matters to me personally.

i can see now that this one issue actually does represent my purpose and the big why that drives what i do.

i believe that we each have a light we are meant to shine in this world.

you deserve to shine that light. you deserve the freedom to BE YOU and STAND TALL and shine in whatever way you want!

how DARE someone tell you otherwise, based on their own agenda (be it political, religious, business, or personal)?

LGBTQ equality and acceptance gets me fired up because it is about being YOU. embracing YOU. sharing your voice. shining your light. living the life that you are born to live. loving yourself exactly as you are. feeling worthy. feeling confident. feeling authentic.

it's about NOT hiding anymore. not allowing your light to be dimmed or extinguished. because life is too fucking short to be anyone but exactly who you are.

that is what my mission is about, helping women every single day remember and believe in and express their soul's purpose... to own their light in this world. and so, to see any soul being told that who they are is not allowed, not accepted, not valued... well, it pisses me off.

it's not ok.

are there other things that i care about? absolutely! over the years i've been passionate about many things: environmentalism and sustainability, feminism and women's rights, public education and support for public teachers... just to name a few. i've always been willing to fight for what i believe in.

but i know now that my job isn't to fight every battle that there is.

mine is to empower and inspire women to step up and fight the battles that they give one huge fuck about. to raise their voice, to be visible, and to shine a light on that one thing that really drives them... their purpose, their why, their mission.

this is my purpose. to help others find and fight for theirs. this is what i am really passionate about.

imagine a world where we all felt strong enough, empowered enough to come forward and say...

"here i am world. this is me. this is what i want the world to know. this is what i want to shine a light on. i am done hiding. i am done being small and insignificant and inauthentic. i am here to shine, exactly as i am."

and the best part is that you don't have to wait... you can start now. start today. open your blog or your email or your favourite social platform, and share your message.

your fight doesn't have to be massive. you don't have to change the whole world. but you can change ONE world. you can change the world for one person, in some way, with whatever it is you do.

so please, give one huge fuck.

decide what you are here to fight for. what would you get up on your soapbox about? what would you talk about passionately given any opportunity? what moves you, deeply, to tears, anger, curiosity, laughter, confusion, frustration, bliss? what is your fight song?

these things can be signposts to your purpose and your why and can help you to ignite your light. they can also be the things that you need to share more with others - they are the messages you can beam out to the world.

gabby bernstein says: "*when you are moved by your message, your message moves the masses.*"[8]

get moved. get fired up. find the mission that is bigger than you, bigger than the stuff you do, bigger than the job you have or the business you build, bigger than your passions and interests.

spreading a message about your mission feels way more authentic, natural, and fun than sharing a message about who you are or what you do. your mission ignites you and connects you to others who care about the same stuff you do.

let your mission be your message.

your manifesto

back when i first started the *build a little biz* blog i created a little manifesto for myself which was a declaration that 'i am a little biz builder'.

at the time, so much of what i was seeing about starting a small business just didn't feel like it was for me; it didn't feel applicable to a mum who was doing this on her own from her kitchen table in between breastfeeding and playgroup!

my purpose for starting that blog was to share what i was learning about business but flipping it into some format that would actually work for women like me and little businesses like mine.

i realized that i needed to stop comparing my journey to what so many other business owners were doing, and i needed to own my journey... i needed to believe in myself and what it meant to me to be building that business.

and so the 'i am a little biz builder' manifesto was created to remind myself WHY i was doing what i was doing, as well as help me keep my eyes on my path... i did it to stay true to myself.

i shared my little manifesto on the blog and was really glad to see that it resonated with many others... it was downloaded and shared quite widely, and i also handed out printed copies any time i went to a live event or meetup.

a few very cool things happened when i shared that manifesto: i was reminded that i was part of an awesome community of women that felt the same way i did; women visiting my site knew they were in the right place for them; and we were able to connect in a much deeper way because we were con-connecting to our why and our purpose.

i went on to create other manifestos as well. the next was a companion to the first, called 'i love my little biz,' which for me was a way to take ownership of the word 'little' because i was tired of feeling like it was equated with 'less than.'

and then when i started the lighthouse revolution i created a video manifesto to inspire people to think about the business they were building in a new way... to not just build a business but build a *lighthouse* business.

a manifesto is a wonderful way to get really clear on what *you* care about and why. it is a wonderful way to let *other* people know what you care about and why. and it is a wonderful way to connect with those people that feel the same!

a manifesto can be written as a book, it can be presented as a poster, it can be done as a video or a slide show or even a photograph. there are no rules here! you can have a bit of fun making a manifesto for your business or your family or your career or your home or your community... whatever it is that lights up your purpose!

consider these questions: what do i stand for? what do i believe in? what is the change i want to make in the world (or in my world)?

what would your manifesto say?

your brand

i've spent quite a lot of time learning about and teaching about branding and i have come to the conclusion that even if you do not have a business, every single one of us could benefit from thinking about ourselves as a brand.

your brand is the message you send out to the world about who you are, what you stand for, what your promise is, what you want to be known for. it should be clear and consistent and simple - everyone should get the same vibe no matter how or when they come into contact with you?

imagine if you had to brand YOU?

would your brand be bold, bright, vibrant? would it be simple, zen, minimalist? would it be quirky, fun, whimsical? would it be no-nonsense, professional, organized?

and what is it about you that sends off that vibe?

the way you speak, the clothes you wear, the accessories you choose, the way you interact with people, the stuff you post on social media, the music/books/art/shows you rave about... all of it sends off a vibe.

as i was building my personal brand i spent some time thinking about the vibe i wanted and how i would portray it. my message has always been that you are here to be you, but the lighthouse soon became the symbol i would use to convey that message - it became my signature thing. along with anything beach or sea related, anything aqua coloured, and anything related to the words light or lighthouse.

remember the poem about wearing purple and a red hat? that has become a signature thing for many women - in fact there are 'red hat society' clubs formed around the world!

sometimes a signature thing will identify you to others who care about the same things you care about. i am a huge fan of the TV show *supernatural* - there are a few different symbols or signature things associated with that show, but when one of us sees it on another person there is always a moment of 'hey, i see you. you're awesome.'

what is your signature thing? and how does it represent who you are, your purpose, your vision, your passion... your light?

your signature thing can be anything: a colour, a word or a phrase, an object, a shape or a pattern, a song even!

imagine if you were starting a club for people who are into the same stuff you are... what symbol would represent your club?

imagine if you were going to get a tattoo as a representation of your light... your soul. or imagine going to an event and having the chance to hand out temporary tattoos that matched your passion or your mission or your message... what would that tattoo be?

imagine if your friends were to call you the _____ lady or the queen of _____ - how would they fill in those blanks?

what are you known for? what do you want to be known for? what is your signature thing?

own who you are. say boldly and out loud: *hey world, this is me.*

connect

i know it can be really hard to beam our light out... to share what we do with others. we struggle with self-doubt. we wonder if we are enough. we wonder who would even care. we have fears and blocks that leave us feeling stuck.

i recently had an extraordinary opportunity to talk with a group of wise soul guides who came through to answer one burning question i had, and so i asked about the feelings of unworthiness that so many women in business are struggling with.

here is their message to me, which i wanted to share with you.

what if you stopped thinking about yourself?

what if instead you think of that one person that you are here to serve or help?

can you picture that one person?

imagine her sitting alone on a single chair in a dark room... in a world that is not making sense right now. feeling isolated, lost, frustrated, annoyed, confused, overwhelmed, ineffective, lonely (or any of those other horrible things any one of us is struggling with.)

what does it feel like for her?

the pain. the despair. the disconnect.

feel that now.

what can you do for her?

i think you already know exactly what she needs.

can you step up from your chair and walk across to her? can you wrap her in a warm blanket, offer her a hug, let her know she is not alone?

yes, there is a gap you must cross. a comfort zone. a fear that you will be criticised. a voice that says you might fail. a feeling deep inside that you are not enough.

but you must step over that gap. you must cross that threshold.

find your one person. go out to her.

take your heart to her heart.

nothing else matters, only your connection to her.

when you do this, not only will you make a difference to her, but to many others like her. and you will also make a difference to YOU.

this is the thing about being a beacon - even though you are sharing your stories and talking about your own journey, and sharing your passion with others, it's not actually *all* about *you*.

it's about that human soul on the other side of your message.

it's about connecting... your heart to their heart.

true connection comes when both people feel seen and heard and valued. it's about both giving and receiving.

here is a really interesting thing about being a lighthouse that we can sometimes forget:

there is a sort of romantic notion about the lighthouse - how beautiful and significant they are, standing out in the landscape with their light shining bright.

but what we must remember is that, in a storm, the lighthouse is not actually the hero of the story. the captain of the ship is!

when you share your light, when you communicate and connect with others, you are helping someone else be the hero of *their* story, of their journey, of their storm.

what can you do today to help someone else be the hero of their story?

your boats

when you speak up, when you are visible, when you stand tall and stand out... sometimes:

people won't like it; people won't like you; people will talk about you behind your back; people will criticise you; people will disagree with you; people will hate that you shine bright; people won't notice you at all; people won't care what you have to say; people will copy you; people will leave you and move onto something or someone else.

and i know that it's really hard when these things happen. and i know that when we fear these things happening it can block us from owning and sharing our light with others.

but what if nothing bad happened at all? or what if, even if something bad happened, it was worth it!

what if:

you made a difference to just one other person; you were noticed by just the right person to help propel your success; you helped someone, greatly; you gained new, avid friends and fans; your message reached the exact person who's been longing to find someone like you; your message went viral; you reached a tipping point; you had a positive impact; you felt ignited and authentic and on purpose.

perhaps, if you make an effort to raise your visibility and raise your voice, one or more of these things will happen.

but for sure, NONE of it will happen if you don't.

your comfort zone is safe. and it feels good. and it would be really nice to keep coasting (or hiding! or playing small.)

but if you want something awesome to happen, you have to do something awesome. you have to be visible and bold and bright.

because your voice in this space matters. there is someone out there who needs to hear what you have to say or see what it is you do.

sure, someone might not like it when you speak up. but let's not give that person more energy than they deserve.

instead focus on the person who will absolutely love it... she is just waiting to find out about you or connect with you in some way.

focus on your boats!

we must remember that not every boat needs a lighthouse. not every boat wants a lighthouse. some boats couldn't care less about the lighthouse!

it's not your job to be everything to everyone all of the time.

it's your job to be you. to be your own lighthouse. and to focus on your boats.

so when someone doesn't like you, or is not into you, or doesn't care about the same stuff you do, or tells you they think you are crazy or wrong or weird or whatever...

remember that what they think about you is none of your business.

and focus on your boats.

amplify your beam

as i began to share the message of the lighthouse i felt like i was *always* talking about the lighthouse. i was blogging about the lighthouse. i was sharing lighthouse images and quotes all over social media. i was talking about it whenever i was at a meet up or event.

it seemed like i was going on and on about this new passion of mine; i worried that i was beginning to sound like a broken record and i worried that i was beginning to annoy people.

and then one night, i had a quick chat with an online friend over skype - this is someone i had been following closely as i really admire the work does and i just love following her stuff - and she said: "what have you been up to lately?"

she hadn't heard or seen a thing about the light-house revolution!

just because i knew everything that was going on with her i assumed she'd seen just as much from me.

just because i had been sharing my stuff in all my usual places i assumed everyone had seen it all already.

that was such a huge eye opener for me... people actually spend very little time thinking about you.

and even if it seems like you are on and on about something (because you have to live with yourself 24/7) to everyone else it is merely a blip on the radar!

you can go on and on about something, but if you are only doing it in the safe, comfy places that you already share stuff, no one new will see it!

to share YOU, to be a beacon and share your light with others, you have to push out of your comfort zone.

if it feels comfy and safe and easy you are probably not being bold enough... YOU enough.

for instance, if you share something with your bestie and that feels safe but you haven't shared it any-where else, or with anyone else, it could be a sign that you aren't really beaming your light very far beyond the shore. it could be a sign that it's time to give your light a little signal boost so that it can actually leave the shore.

and a funny thing happens when you start to amplify your beam... soon what was once pretty bold and 'out there' now becomes the new 'comfy and safe.'

keep pushing out of your comfort zone. honour your light by sharing it with others.

be vulnerable

sharing YOU... connecting with others and opening up about who you are and the things you care about and the stories that have shaped you... being authentic and real and raw... this stuff feels really vulnerable.

it *is* really vulnerable.

as the amazing brené brown says: *"vulnerability is the courage to show up and be seen."*[9] and that is what being a beacon is all about... being seen.

there is one thing i have noticed as i have carried on my own journey down this road... when we allow ourselves to be vulnerable, amazing things happen.

and usually, the thing we are most worried about happening as a consequence of being vulnerable doesn't happen at all. then, if it does, we surprise ourselves by how well we survive it, how the whole world doesn't actually fall apart.

i have experienced this over and over again.

the day that i shared my thoughts on LGBTQ rights over on my blog, i had a moment after i clicked publish when i thought perhaps it would be easier if i just didn't make a big deal about what i had written... if i just kept it kind of quiet, you know?

it's funny how we can fool ourselves into thinking we are doing so well with shining our light. i wrote this big, ranty, controversial post, clicked publish, patted myself on my back for my bravery and awesomeness, and then was quite prepared to walk away without having actually shared what i wrote with anyone!

it was not the actual *writing* of the post, but the idea of *sharing* the post widely that triggered my fear, made me feel vulnerable and open to attack.

so i forced myself out of my comfort zone, sent the post via email to my mailing list, posted it on all of my social media accounts, and popped into a few online forums to share it there too.

within minutes i had a seemingly unrelated email from a new client asking for a full refund on a big package she had recently purchased, stating that she no longer wished to work with me.

there was no reason to believe the two were related, she didn't tell me *why* she didn't want to work with me, she didn't call me out on my opinion or disagree with me or say anything against my values.

but in my gut, i knew it was because of my ranty post.

i was devastated. i felt like i had taken this big risk to talk openly about something that really mattered to me, to take a stand and raise my voice, and i felt like the universe rewarded me with a huge loss in income!

yuck. it felt pretty awful.

and then the most amazing things began to happen.

i had so many messages of thanks from people who felt that i had put into words exactly what they had been feeling.

i had new people reach out to connect with me - adding me to their groups, sharing my post even more widely, helping me to raise my visibility.

and i remembered that i needed to focus on *my boats*. if that client no longer felt like she was in the right place it was *good* that she asked for a refund before i had invested any time or energy into working with her.

it was a beautiful clean break, with no hard feelings (on my side at least), and i sent her a refund with nothing but love.

try making note of the times when you feel incredibly vulnerable and what happens when you take action anyway. i bet that you begin to notice what i do - amazing things happen (even if the amazing thing is that nothing bad happens at all!)

and no matter what action you take - what story you share, what soapbox you jump on, what boats you connect with, what vulnerability you experience - remember this...

do all things from a place of love.

it might seem cliché but i honestly think this makes the biggest difference.

sometimes when we are in a position to share our light with others - by helping others, by teaching or leading or guiding others, by volunteering or working or selling something, even just by talking about the stuff we care deeply about - ego can get really loud.

we can begin to concentrate on what we stand to gain (or lose, as was the case with my client refund), we consider how beaming our light will serve *us* best, or we find ourselves in a place that feels awfully self-absorbed.

in those times, try to remember that love is the thing.

speak with love. send love out. be open to receiving love. find the little nuggets of love in your stories and connections.

when love is your intention your light is pure and true.

being a beacon means sharing YOU... sharing your light and allowing it to beam outwards. it's about speaking your truth, declaring yourself... saying hey world, this is me. it's about communication and connection. being seen and heard and seeing and hearing others too... witnessing their light as you shine yours.

build your tower.

serve you.

seek alignment & integrity.

choose simplicity.

give yourself permission.

do it your way.

build what you love.

love your light.

part 3

build your tower

the tower of the lighthouse represents the life that you are actually building for yourself... it's the structure, or the vehicle, that allows you to be you and to shine your light in the world.

and the fact is, we all have a structure that we have built for ourselves already, without even realizing it!

our lives are full of all sorts of *stuff* - work and relationships and activities and belongings and obligations and and and.

some of it wonderful, some of it perhaps not quite so.

the lighthouse reminds us to build a tower.

something which aligns with who you are... with your purpose and your vision; something that will leverage your strengths and your passions; something with strength and integrity where every component belongs.

what you are building has to match who you are. it needs to serve you well. it needs to love your light.

integrity & alignment

the definition of integrity that we tend to think of first is the quality of being honest & fair; having strong moral principles. and i definitely think this is important in life... to be who we say we are, and to do what we say we'll do.

but another definition of integrity keeps coming to mind as i think about the lighthouse we are here to build: *the state of being complete & whole. unimpaired. sound. solid.*

and alignment means: *in agreement. give support. each component lines up with the others.*

how is the integrity & alignment of your tower?

have a look around you. what are you surrounded by? what are you busy doing? what's on your to do list? what's in your calendar?

your tower is made up of all of the *stuff* in your life.

jobs. work. study. hobbies. activities. belongings. physical spaces. obligations. tasks. strategies. plans. responsibilities. money. spiritual practices. people. relationships.

and often, as time goes on, our life can get cluttered up with an awful lot of stuff.

how well is all of that stuff serving you?

remember your BIG vision? that dream you have for yourself? that role you wish to play? that purpose you are here to live?

does your *stuff* line up with all of that?

because here is the thing: over time we evolve. we are supposed to! we grow and change and learn and adapt and grow some more.

yet, so often, our physical world doesn't really reflect the person we wish to be. instead it reflects who we've been up until now.

we do things because we feel like we should or because it's just what we have always done. we have things we've accumulated along the way. our world gets fuller and fuller of *stuff* (physical stuff, emotional stuff, stuff on our to do lists, stuff that weighs us down).

when i think of the tower of the lighthouse, all of that *stuff* makes it feel really wobbly - like i can barely hold it all together, like it could all come crumbling down in a moment, like i am stuck in the basement and i can't make my way through it all to get to my light at the top.

when we get rid of all of the stuff that no longer serves us, no longer lights us up, no longer aligns with who we wish to be... we make space for something new, something more, something even better.

and damn does it feel good!

here is what i've decided about the life i am building for myself. if there is something in my space that is sucking the light right out of me, it has got to change.

and if i can't change it, then i have to change the way i think about it.

let's say for instance, i decide to start running for exercise because that is what someone suggests i *should* do or it's what my friends are *all* doing or maybe it's what i've *always* done so i just keep on running.

but i hate running. it really does suck the light out of me. so what i need to do is give myself permission to throw running right out the window of my lighthouse.

do something else. do something that lights me up. try yoga. or dancing. or biking. or walking. or tennis. i don't know! i might not know until i try it... but we only have so much time and energy and focus and money to spend... let's spend it on something that lights us up (and meets the goal of exercise too!)

ok, now let's say i hate my job. it is also something that is sucking the light right out of me. that one is a bit trickier to throw out the window. let's face it - we need to earn money so that we can take care of ourselves and our families and so we can build the life that will light us up.

so in this case, what i need to do is change the way i think about it. i need to find a way to feel aligned with that job, to make it fit into my tower, to light it up in some way.

one of my favourite ways to do this is to find the one thing about the job that really does light me up, that allows me to feel on purpose (even in a tiny way) or that helps me focus on that BIG vision i have for myself... to find that little pocket of light in the shadows.

looking back, i can see ways that i have done this without realizing it. when i was coaching women in biz about their branding and marketing, our conversations would inevitably end up being around who they were in the world, how they see themselves and share themselves with others, what their purpose and their mission was... that was the stuff that really lit me up!

and eventually i gave myself permission to make some changes to my work and my offerings so that i could do more of that stuff. eventually i gave myself permission to stop doing the work or jobs that didn't light me up any more.

permission is a pretty powerful thing!

and it is essential to building your tower.

permission to declutter the crap. permission to make a change. permission to simplify. permission to add whatever has been missing.

give yourself permission to replace the stuff that sucks the light right out of you with something that lights you up instead!

"house" rules

who says? is one of my favourite mantras.

(but in my head i actually say *who the fuck says?* or sometimes even *WTFS?* because it feels more powerful that way! of course you don't have to swear if it's not your thing.)

this mantra is one that i need to remind myself of often.

sometimes i seem to forget that i am the boss of my life. i will be going along, feeling stuck or frustrated or wobbly, and then i will remember... oh yah. that's right...

who says?

because, here is the thing:

YOU are the keeper of your lighthouse. you are the builder of your lighthouse. you ARE your lighthouse.

and that means that you need to do it *your way*. you need to do what feels right for you. what fits. what aligns. what serves.

so in your life, start asking this question...

who says?

whenever you are told by someone:

> you can't do it that way.
>
> you must do it this way.
>
> you should do this.
>
> you should never do that.
>
> you need to have this.
>
> you better get rid of that.
>
> you don't have enough of this.
>
> you are too much of that.
>
> this is the way.
>
> this is the path.
>
> these are the steps you need to take.
>
> these are the rules.

... well you get the idea i think!

before i go on... i do get that there *are* some very valuable rules to follow. we *can* absolutely learn from others. we can of course follow steps and strategies and examples. and there is nothing wrong with seeking out help whenever we need it!

i am not at all saying we throw out *all* the advice we ever receive. but what i encourage is this:

practice saying: *"who says?"*

and then go back to you. look inside... check your inner compass.

what feels like you? what is doable for you? what is sustainable for you? what matches who you are and the work you are here to do and the life you are building and the message you want to send and the people you truly want to help?

it's all got to fit!

you might need to break the rules. you might need to write your own rules. you might need to be a trailblazer.

you might need to give yourself permission to say NO. or say yes. or make a change. to start something new. or stop something because it doesn't fit any more. or do things in a way that make the most sense for you.

you might also need to define things your way.

i remember when i first started helping women in business i did not feel like a 'coach'... that word just did not sit right with me. (i think it reminds me too much of physical education class in school and playing team sports and that makes me shudder!)

i couldn't think of what to call myself, what title i was meant to have... nothing fit. after some googling, thesaurus searching, and brainstorming i decided to make up my own word: unstucktor. now *that* felt like me! i help women get unstuck. i am an unstucktor!

when i first thought about myself as a teacher again, it felt liberating. it felt like me! but it also brought up some *stuff*. i remember when i was working as a schoolteacher being told by someone that it was a shame that i was *'just'* a teacher. as though being a teacher were not enough!

i realized that i had to take back that word - teacher - and redefine it for me now... for my life and my BIG vision.

i also remember one day when i was feeling particularly stressed, a friend suggested that i needed some balance: "you need to go out and get some exercise, you need to sit and have a cup of tea, you need to take a long hot bath, and go to bed early!"

she was very well meaning, and absolutely said it from a place of love, but when i heard that i nearly snapped!

first of all, most of those things don't even appeal to me. secondly, i had a toddler at home... most of those things weren't even achievable.

after i got over my silly rage i realized that was how *she* defined and achieved balance. i needed to find my own way, my own strategies... my own definition of balance that suited me!

it's your tower... you need to be able to own it. you need to be able to live in it. comfortably and with enthusiasm.

so you might need to rewrite the dictionary - you decide how a word should be defined for you, and which words you choose to define yourself and your life.

you might need to toss a word right out the window - never to let it define you ever again.

you might need to invent your own words or definitions or titles. why not?

your words have power. choose wisely!

and remember that whatever you choose - you aren't doing it wrong.

if you are a teacher or a coach or an entrepreneur or anything else... you aren't doing it wrong. if you are on a spiritual journey, or a health journey, or a learning journey, or a healing journey... you aren't doing it wrong. if you choose one strategy over another, one pathway over another, one activity over another... you aren't doing it wrong.

i know that sometimes we want someone just to give us the steps, give us the formula or the magic pill so we can follow along and 'get it right.' this is your tower, your lighthouse, your journey - it needs to work for you.

there is no 'right,' there is just you... what works for you.

so try to let go of getting it right. get into your heart and see what feels right to you, and do it your way.

boundaries

how are your boundaries?

boundaries are not walls. they are not meant to divide or create barriers between you and others. boundaries are simply about honouring yourself... your light... deciding for yourself "this is what is ok."

at the core, setting boundaries is really about giving yourself permission to say NO. or to say yes only when you just know that saying yes will absolutely light you up!

i can remember when i first started my photography business, being really shit at boundaries. maybe it was because for the first time i had no one to answer to but myself. i had no boss telling me what to do. i had no manual with everything spelled out for me. i was trying to find my way on my own.

and that is both liberating and challenging!

i felt like i should say yes to everything and everyone... to every opportunity, to every client, to every request, to every strategy.

it wasn't long before i learned that i had to create some boundaries... to draw some lines in the sand.

because of the way my brain works - the way i like to write everything out and put everything together in a way that clicks - i opened up a blank document and started figuring out my boundaries... writing it all down as though it was the 'official manual' that spelled everything out for my biz.

i wrote down which jobs i would say yes to and which i would say no to. i figured out what my friends and family discount would be and when i would apply it. i decided how many vouchers or freebies i would be willing to give away when asked for charities and fundraisers. i even thought about when i would protect my 'work time' and when i would be willing to be flexible (to say, go for a coffee with my friend, or help out at the school.)

there was something so powerful about writing it all out!

when a friend would ask for a photo session i could refer to the manual and copy and paste the pre-pared text. when someone asked me if they could pick my brain, i could answer within my boundaries.

it was incredibly liberating; if it's written down then it becomes something you just do... you don't have to angst over it any more.

as different situations come up, as i experience different things, as i learn from my mistakes, i can keep adding to the 'official manual'.

i will ask: is this the best use of me? (my time? my energy? my focus? my money?) could someone else do it faster/easier/with more passion and pizazz? is this my zone of genius?

now that is an empowering phrase! if you haven't read the book *the big leap* by gay hendricks,[10] i highly recommend it... it's life changing stuff. one of the things he talks about is how we all have differ-ent zones: incompetence, competence, excellence, and genius. i love this idea: the zone of genius feels like something we need to honour and protect... to choose to only do what only *you* can do.

now, when i get asked to do a job, or help out with something, or volunteer my time, or participate in something someone is planning... i will answer: "thank you for thinking of me, but that isn't really my zone of genius. i hope you find just the right person!" for some reason it feels really comfortable to say it that way.

but you can also simply just say no. *"no."* is a complete sentence.

boundaries are not just for what people ask of you, they are also for how people treat you. it's up to you to decide what is ok, and then honour that by standing your ground, being the bodyguard or the protector of your light.

i try to come from a place of compassion rather than a place of judgement when i am dealing with people, especially people who frustrate me. i choose to believe that people are doing the best they can, with where they are at and with what they have... and i often repeat that in my head in difficult situations.

but i also get to decide when someone's "best" is simply not good enough for me. it's ok to say: i believe she is doing her best, this is her best right now, but her best is still not enough... and so i shall stand up for myself, i shall stand my ground.

we can create boundaries in a variety of ways: with our words and our actions, with how we treat ourselves and others, with distance or space, even with the connections we choose to foster versus those we choose to sever.

our boundaries can be physical, verbal, emotional, even energetic. often times just deciding that we need to create a boundary is enough for things to change, and standing up for ourselves even once is often enough to create a big shift.

it helps me to think of all of these little things as part of the 'official owner's manual' for my light-house.

and that is the thing to remember at the end of the day... i am the lighthouse keeper. no one else is going to tell me what to do! i am the boss, the CEO of my own life. i get to decide. i need to choose. i must build my lighthouse, my way. i must protect my light.

currency

imagine you have a bank account that you get to use to decorate your lighthouse. you go out shopping and walk into a shop filled with the ugliest rugs; so you buy one. next door is a shop with horrendous lamps; you buy a few. you carry on to the shops down the street and purchase furniture that you absolute loath, bedding that makes your skin itch, and dishes that you will probably never use... spending more and more from your account each time.

you've just filled up your lighthouse with items that you absolutely hate, rather than stuff that you love. it's a crazy idea isn't it? why would we ever do that? but we do it all the time...

the currency in that bank account? it is your time, energy, focus, thoughts, and yes, even money, that you spend every single day.

when i was thinking of doing the writing challenge to write this book, my first thought was: *i can't. i don't have the time!* but then i thought about it a little more and came to the conclusion that i was never going to *have* the time unless i created the time. i had to value writing the book more than something else in my life. and i had to make time for it right in my schedule so that i really could focus on writing every single day. so i gave up watching TV in the evenings, which is normally my down time, and wrote every single night from 8 pm. and you know, i didn't even miss my TV!

what will you give up so that you can do the stuff you say you love... the stuff that lights you up... the stuff that you say you want more of in your lighthouse?

your time, your focus, your energy... it is all currency. how are you spending it? and why are you spending it on stuff that doesn't love your light? obligation? someone told you to? perhaps you are avoiding something that scares you?

when i first started talking about the lighthouse revolution i did it from my *build a little biz* platform. i kept offering the same services and products i always had, i kept my business rolling along, and i just snuck in some of this new stuff on the blog where i could.

it didn't take long before i realized that although my business products and services were bringing in money, they were actually costing me much more in the long run. that work no longer felt aligned, i no longer felt like i was leveraging my strengths, and i felt like that 'old' biz was taking up all of my time, energy, and focus, when i really wanted to be putting it in new directions.

however, i hung on to *build a little biz* for nearly another year before making a change. it was starting to suck the light right out of me, and i had a strong sensation that i had this low ceiling overhead that i just couldn't bust through... but i still felt like i couldn't let it go.

sometimes we keep investing our 'currency' in something because we feel a sense of grief, pain, or loss at the thought of giving it up... it would just cost too much to make a change. that is how i felt for a long time with *build a little biz*; it had been my baby, and it was a beloved brand that helped so many people, so i felt guilty shutting the doors. i felt like maybe i was letting myself down somehow by not figuring out how to make it keep working.

in the end i came to the decision by asking myself: if i were my own client what would i recommend they do? what would the lighthouse teach us in this situation? my answer was clear: i knew i needed to stop investing in something that no longer fit inside my lighthouse tower. i knew i needed a clean and clear slate to build something that would be in service of my light, something that i would love and that would love my light.

and so i shut the doors on *build a little biz* and started up a new site under my own personal brand. once i made the decision, the sense of loss dissipated... i actually felt much lighter and more free, like everything that i had done before was no longer holding me back or weighing me down, and the sensation of the ceiling overhead disappeared.

where you invest your currency - your love, your energy, your time, your focus - that is where you invest your life. choose wisely!

as an aside... since we were talking about ugly furniture for this little analogy, it brings to mind one other thing: the actual, physical space of your tower matters too! it is so important to feel that you have a sacred space in your life - a place filled with stuff that you truly do love - a beautiful spot where you feel lit up: physically, mentally, emotionally, and spiritually.

when i first started my businesses from home i would often just sit on the lounge room sofa with my laptop in hand and a baby in my lap. and that was fine, for a while. but as i started to build my lighthouse and find a new level of fulfilment in my work i began to crave a sacred space of my own. eventually i took over a space in our home which is now the headquarters of the lighthouse revolution. i am literally surrounded by lighthouses because i have received so many gorgeous gifts and artworks over the years, and i am surrounded by things that i love, things that love my light, things that serve me well.

whatever a sacred space looks like for you... please take steps to create it. this is a worthy investment of your space and your time... you deserve to have a space where you can find yourself and connect to your light.

lighthouse rooms

last year i was working on a huge project (on a deadline that i was accountable for) and i was feeling totally stuck: i just couldn't sit down and get it done, i kept procrastinating and getting distracted, i was feeling uninspired for ideas.

you know the feeling, right?

i was talking to my mastermind group about how i was struggling and one of the girls said "well what about that lighthouse stuff you have been planning on talking about?"

and i got all excited and animated (as i always do when talking about the lighthouse revolution) and proceeded to tell her all of my plans for it, but said: "first i have to get this project done. *then* i can do that lighthouse stuff."

she said, "well can't you do this AND that?"

but. but. but!

i had many excuses for why not. none of them mattered. i had delegated all of the stuff that really lit me up into the back room and i shut the door on it.

i did the same thing when planning to write this book. i kept talking about how i wanted to write a book and get all of the stuff i had learned about building a lighthouse down onto the page... but i never actually made time to write.

i kept waiting to work on THIS after i finished all of that other stuff i just *had* to do first. i'm sure you can guess... it was never going to be the perfect time.

when we don't make time for the stuff that calls to us, the stuff that makes our heart sing, the stuff that we would do even if we didn't get paid, the stuff that the universe keeps nudging and nudging us to do... when we shove it all away in the back room and shut the door on it all... we totally block the flow for everything.

the reality is that we might truly be on a deadline, or might absolutely have to get some things in place before we can properly focus on that other thing... but you *can* still make some room for it. we can seek a balance between the stuff we have to do and the stuff we need to do.

i went home from that conversation with my mastermind and grabbed a notebook and gave myself 30 minutes to brainstorm some ideas for the lighthouse revolution. after that, i was able to focus on the big project with the deadline.

i joined a writing challenge to get this book written - with a goal to write a set number of words each day until it was done. i made just a little time and space each day to devote to the book - the rest of the day was for all of the other jobs i had to do every day.

as long as i keep the flow going of the stuff that lights me up, i keep the flow going in the other parts of my life as well.

so the next time you find yourself pushing the ideas that excite you into a back room to be dealt with later, or saying: i have to do that (insert thing you don't really love but *have* to do) and THEN i can do this (insert thing you really *love* which ignites your spark and lights you up from within.)

please give yourself permission to do both... *this AND that.*

you don't have to wait for everything to be perfect, or for the timing to be just right, or for all your ducks to be in a row.

talk about it. brainstorm it. plan it. dream it. open up the doors and make some room for it.

let it flow instead of blocking it out or pushing it aside or shutting it away.

i bet the other work you are doing will flow better too.

lighthouse doors

sometimes when we are in the zone of doing what we love and exploring what lights us up we can end up giving a lot of ourselves to others... but it is so important as we beam our light outwards that we do not close our doors to receiving light, love, and abundance in return.

part of our job as we become the keepers of our lighthouse is to ensure that the energy flows both ways: to be open to both giving and receiving... to be sure that abundance is able to flow both from you and back to you.

for some reason this seems to be a trouble spot for so many of us who are shining our light. when we embrace our gifts, and live our purpose, and start sharing with others what so naturally lights us up, we seem to think that we should not expect anything in return.

this seems to be especially true of women who are building a business based on their purpose... it seems quite challenging for so many of us to believe that we deserve to earn money for work that we are doing because it absolutely ignites our soul.

but i think it is true in *all* areas of life - whether in our homes, our communities, our workplaces - the stuff that lights us up is the stuff we would be doing naturally anyhow and we just can't help but share it with others... even if we were never paid for it, or sometimes even acknowledged for it.

not to say that money is the only type of abundance that we need to be open to - abundance can flow in many different ways. and when we close the door to receiving we create an uneven energy in our lighthouse... the light is always beaming out but we have nothing coming into us in return.

we must be sure to open our doors up wide and become just as adept at receiving as we are at giving: whether that energy exchange comes in the form of money, or time, or gratitude, or assistance, or support, or thanks, or appreciation, or kindness, or love, or any other form of abundance!

denise duffield-thomas[11] has a fantastic mantra that i would like to borrow to post up on the lighthouse wall: *i serve, i deserve.* being in the zone of shining your light: connecting with others, being of service, beaming your light out and sharing your gifts does NOT mean that you do not deserve anything in return.

in fact, that is an unsustainable situation. as we have already said: you need fuel in your tanks if you are to keep on shining. allowing abundance into your life means that you can keep doing what lights you up, you can keep shining for a long time to come. if you give everything you've got to your light and you do not receive anything in return the whole thing is going to burn right out... and you will be back where you started, feeling incredibly unsatisfied.

so shine your light indeed... be generous with your gifts and your passions. but also open your doors to receiving love and light in return, and receive it with grace and gratitude. there is nothing classier than to be someone who both gives freely and receives graciously.

lighthouse walls

it happens sometimes... things are swimming along, you are doing the work, you are doing ok. then bam! a negative comment shows up in your inbox or newsfeed or even in a face to face interaction.

a common one for me is the no capitals thing. here is a recent email i received:

"just FYI, if you want to build a business, you might want to start using proper capitalization. while trendy, it doesn't sit well with the *real* business crowd. best of luck to you."

and here's another one from when i wrote a blog post and created a quote image with a direct quote from a famous spiritual leader that included the phrase "fucking unstoppable."

"sending me an email with the "F"word in it is sad! you don't need to be a 'coach' if this is how you talk!!!"

these could easily be any comments, from anyone - the point is that when you get them, they do sting! i know we've all experienced them:

a complaint about something you shared, a criticism of the way you do (or don't) do something, an offside comment about something you worked hard on, a dig at something you really care about, a snide remark about how you are wasting your time, or any sort of judgement or dismissal from someone whose opinion you value.

when they happen they feel like a reflection on who you are and the way you live your life.

and when they happen they generally bring up all sorts of yucky fears we have around not being liked, not being approved of, not being good enough, being rejected, being judged.

the first thing to remember is that those comments are generally NOT about you at all - they are more about the person saying them, and their own stuff.

but even knowing that, it can still make you feel pretty shitty. right?

the key is to not let that stuff become permanent graffiti all over your walls.

just picture that for a second. let's say you've just worked your ass off building a gorgeous picket fence around your beautiful garden. you sit out and absolutely love the view in front of you - you feel pride in your home and in the work you did to create that.

then some jackass comes along with spray paint and tags the whole thing. it is so irritating! now every time you look out you see that damned horrible black graffiti - your eyes don't even pick up on the pretty garden or the cute fence.

negative comments can be the same, if you let them. if you keep letting these things take up space in your mind and in your heart, you give them more power than they really have.

so don't let the negative stuff become ugly, permanent graffiti on the thing you are building.

replace it with the positive instead.

write on your walls with love.

and i do mean this literally - grab a piece of paper and write down some awesome, loving, positive stuff instead. there is something powerful in the actual process of writing, and something in having it in front of you to fill your view every day.

i have a giant black board on my wall - it truly feels like the walls of my lighthouse - full of awesome, positive words, doodles, and reminders.

you could grab a chalk pen and write all over your window or mirror. you could get a big poster board and write on it and stick it on your wall. you could use an app on your phone and have reminders pop up every hour. do it any way you like!

what can you write?

awesome feedback from people who love what you do; email or social media comments that made your day; your word of the year; 'i am' statements; affirmations; ah ha moments; any nudges you have been getting to head in a certain direction or do a certain thing; your purpose, your why; permission that you give to yourself; something that ignites your spark; something that keeps you grounded; stuff that lifts you higher.

negative shit is going to happen. it's just life. but you can make the choice to not let that take up permanent space in your life or in your heart.

instead, write on your walls with love.

(p.s. i would love to see what your wall looks like. tag me in a photo on instagram, facebook, or twitter! @karengunton)

lighthouse keeper

who do you surround yourself with? are those people light extinguishers or light igniters?

the reality is that not everyone is going to love this new life you are building for yourself. not everyone is going to get it. in fact some people will feel downright threatened by it - it can be very intimidating and unsettling for some people to be faced with someone who is absolutely owning her light.

and that's ok. it's not your job to convince everyone around you of this new way of thinking about life and what it means to light up.

your job is to quietly go about building your lighthouse. your job is to be the keeper of your lighthouse.

it certainly helps if you have people in your life who love your light, who want to add to it, and of course who want to shine themselves.

part of your job is to seek out these light igniters... your kindred lighthouse keepers who will help you to care for yourself and your lighthouse, who will help you feel safe and supported, who will stand up and shine for you on the days when you feel dim.

chances are you already have a few of these people in your life - as you share more of yourself and start aligning your life, more will appear.

and chances are you also have some of the light extinguishers in your life. the ones who would rather you stay small and dim and the same...

what of those people?

well it's your choice really. there are times when some decluttering of the people and relationships in your life is needed - trust your gut on that! and give yourself permission to move on if that is what you need.

but there are also times where it's not necessary (or practical!) to cut someone out of your life in order to feel more ignited. they don't need to take on the role of lighthouse keeper... you can simply relegate them to other roles.

there are people in my life that just do not get what i do. they aren't negative or anything but they have a way of looking at my work with a sort of blank stare that is a bit disconcerting. i just tend to not talk about my work with them and keep the conversation to other areas that are satisfying to both of us!

i know some people who seem to be in a pretty negative space sometimes - they often talk about how their life is so hard and complicated and sucky (you get the picture) but would rather complain than do anything about it, so those conversations don't really go anywhere! i find it better to do things with them like go to the movies where we don't have to sit around and bitch and moan the whole time.

and i know some people who are downright light extinguishers and clearly can't wait to say some-thing critical or sarcastic or off-putting. i know i have to see them in various situations, no getting out of it, but i don't have to allow that into my life. i picture a little reflective bubble around me and their negativity just bounces off!

i also find it quite fun to be super bright and shiny around people like that - nothing is more confusing to a light extinguisher than when their tactics don't work at all! i also quite like playing a game of bingo in my head - predict everything they will say that is meant to dim your light, and when it happens shout "BINGO" loud in your head! it totally turns the energy around, for you at least!

no matter what, make sure you have regular con-tact with your lighthouse keepers - have a standing date with a bestie who understands what you are working on for yourself, create a little online safe haven for a few like-minded souls and hop on skype together, or have daily check-ins with someone who absolutely loves your light so you can remember that always - and don't be afraid to ask for help when you need it.

your lighthouse keepers are the gorgeous souls in your life who will help you take care of your light.

build what you love

every once in a while i receive hate mail... i see it as just a part of having a public presence with my business and blog, and so i try not to let it get to me.

(in fact i usually celebrate it! you don't get haters if you are bland and boring... but you don't get lovers either! hate mail is a sign that i am amplifying my message.)

one of the first bits of hate mail i ever received was not actually intended as such, it wasn't intended to be sent to me... one of the subscribers to my news-letter hit reply instead of forward when she was sending my email to a friend.

her message went something like this: "omg this woman is so annoying. i can't stand her. but she has some helpful information here, if you can get past her terrible grammar, lack of capitalization, and horrible writing style."

when i first read the message i actually felt really bad for the person who sent it, i could imagine how mortifying it would be to know you sent that to the wrong person!

i considered not replying but i really wanted to share the following message with her (and i did try to do so from a place of love):

build what you love instead of bashing what you hate.

it is such a simple little thing but i feel like far too many of us spend far too much time bemoaning the life we have, complaining about other people, tearing others down, criticising the way others choose to live their life or shine their light.

it's just not necessary. and it holds us back from building up our own lives.

even though that person did not mean to put me down to my face - she never intended that message to be hate mail sent to me - it was still very negative and quite unkind. and it was unnecessary... a simple "she's not really for me but i thought you might like her," would have been fine.

what sort of energy are we putting out to the world when we focus on everything we don't like instead of spending time building up what we love?

the tower of the lighthouse reminds me to build what i love, build what will serve my light.

i actually think it is the ultimate act of self-love to build a tower - something with integrity and purpose, something that aligns with the kind of person i wish to be in the world.

with my tower, i am saying: i love myself enough and i honour my light enough that i am willing to build a life that serves me.

not sure if you are building what you love? just imagine that you had to put onto a giant billboard whatever you are spending all of your focus and energy on. would you be happy for that to happen or would it make you cringe? be sure that you are building exactly what you *want* to build.

build what you love.

build what will serve your light.

build what you need most in this world yourself.

build what will liberate you.

build what lights you up.

and don't spend any more focus, energy, time, or thought on what anyone else is building. if it doesn't suit you - you don't need to tell them! you don't need to bash anyone - to their faces or in private. you don't need to knock anyone down.

don't get me wrong - i do not always stay out of this negative space. i am human, just like anyone, and i can definitely get caught up in the bashing too.

but i am trying to be more aware of it, i am trying to see that it doesn't serve me to be in that space. and i am trying to be reminded by the lighthouse to focus on my own tower before knocking down anyone else's.

are there things that other people do that bug me? that i dislike? that i don't agree with? that rub me the wrong way?

absolutely.

but it's not my work to focus on any of that. it's my work to build a life that will light *me* up. (and i don't need to take away from anyone else's light to do that.)

if i find myself in that negative space of bashing what someone else is building, i will try to catch myself and say instead: "nothing but love for you sister." it reminds me: 'to each their own.' and even if i don't dig it myself, i can walk away from that situation wishing the other person luck with their journey.

let them build their thing - i've got a lighthouse to focus on.

building your tower means carefully choosing exactly what is in your life... filling your life (your space, your body, your work, your relationships, your time) with the stuff that aligns with your vision and serves your light. this is the ultimate act of self-love... building a tower that you love, one that loves your light.

strengthen your foundation.

build you.

believe in yourself.

expand out of your comfort zone.

take action.

stand tall.

back yourself.

support your light.

part 4

strengthen your foundation

the foundation of the lighthouse is there to strengthen and support the entire structure above... the tower, the beacon, the beautiful light.

the foundation is the ground you build on... the rock. it needs to be solid, stable, and strong, in order to support you as you do the work you are here to do, build the life you want to build, and shine the light you are here to shine.

building your foundation means building *you*.

your foundation is made up of a number of building blocks: mindset, confidence, worthiness, belief, commitment, courage, resilience... all of the inner stuff we need to build up in ourselves in order to stand tall and stand out and shine our light.

some building blocks come naturally to us, we can cement them in and make excellent use of them. others we need to build on purpose just as we build any other aspect of our lives...

we need to build ourselves up too, in order to support our light.

mindset

i am sure that you, like me, often see inspiring quote images or blog articles that say something super helpful like: if you want others to value you, you must first value yourself. or perhaps something like: success starts with you, you've got to believe in yourself!

wonderful platitudes that basically tell you that you have to work on you.

and these messages are certainly inspiring, but they often leave me feeling intensely frustrated as well: ok, i get it! we need to feel worthy. we need to have confidence. we need to believe in ourselves. we need to build a strong mindset.

but HOW? no, seriously, how the hell does one just magically start feeling worthy?

maybe that is a product of the way my brain works, the way i need to piece things together to make sense of the world, and make things click. i am always asking questions like... *but how?* and *but why?*

or maybe it was just because of the place i was at in my journey... i had done the external stuff (figured out what i was good at, built a business, got paid for it) and now i was at the phase of realizing i had to do the internal stuff too (hello worthiness, i am looking at you!)

so i set out on this quest to figure out HOW. how exactly does one build the mindset stuff that is so important.

because, as i quickly discovered, the foundation certainly doesn't just magically appear when you start shining your light.

you've actually got to build that part too. no one else is going to suddenly appear to build up your confidence, your worthiness, your sense of deserving. it's part of your job to build this stuff too... to build you.

your ability to stand tall and stand strong depends on you!

so i set out to try to learn HOW... and damned if there is no easy answer! damn. no wonder this inner work is so hard!

when you build a website there is a pretty standard approach to getting it done. same for building an exercise plan or publishing a book. you want to do this sort of stuff - you check with google and get some pretty straight forward answers and check-lists.

when you build *you*? not so much.

what i did discover is that it is often enough to just be aware of what you've got to build.

when you realize: *damn i'm pretty hard on myself. i don't feel like i actually deserve to be happy, or earn money, or spend time on me. what can i do to build myself up, i wonder?*

it's like you flip a switch in the universe somewhere and lessons and strategies and helpful people start to come your way.

at one point on my journey, i was in a place where i was feeling really ineffective and unsuccessful... my confidence had plummeted. i was working with a mentor and she suggested that i need to get out of my head and into my heart (which i will talk some more about later). she suggested i deepen my spiritual practice - connect to myself and my soul. i kind of laughed at that suggestion as i had no spiritual practice to deepen! (unless you count drinking beer at the beach a spiritual practice!)

about two hours later i was waiting to pick up my daughter and got to chatting with another mum in the parking lot. she asked me about my biz, i asked her about hers, and quite randomly she told me that she was going to start offering reiki certification courses. now this was someone i had met many years ago but we never really got to know each other very well - yet on this day we just happened to get into a deep conversation about spiritual practice!

as she was telling me more about reiki i realized it sounded like the exact thing i was looking for and i knew then that our meeting was no accident, so i signed up. that then led me on a path to getting really curious about chakras, which lead me to trying out some different meditations and enjoying it for the first time ever! which let to me playing and exploring further and discovering ways to combine reiki and chakra work and meditation with the lessons of the lighthouse and voila... over time i seemed to have developed my own kind of spiritual practice! (which, by the way, still includes drinking beer by the beach!)

once you are aware of what you need to build and you ask for help building it, the people and tools will show up to help you!

the other thing i've realized as i've been talking with so many women over the years about their purpose and their dreams for themselves: we each have our own stuff to build.

i spend a lot of time in various online groups for entrepreneurs. when i was first working on building my business i noticed that sometimes i would be talking with other women in business who seemed to have great difficulty just taking action, getting shit done, and putting stuff out there. as you will learn - i don't have that problem. i am very comfortable just going for it and putting stuff out there in all of its imperfect glory! and so i would be the one in the group cheering people on saying: "it's not a tattoo! just do it!!"

but then at other times i would marvel at how some women would just create something and put a high price tag on it and go out there and sell it with all of the confidence in the world. that was so hard for me! i would be the one in the group feeling not very confident in my offering, not very confident that people would buy.

once i started studying how to build my foundation i had more understanding that we each have strengths that already exist which we can use to our advantage... we can cement them into our foundation in a big way to make it even stronger!

and we each have building blocks that just do not come naturally to us. we need to make a point of learning HOW to build those aspects in ourselves, so that we may actually stand tall and shine.

which building blocks have you already got, and which do you need to build in?

certainty

one of the foundation blocks i have been really curious to learn how to build is the unwavering belief in oneself that so many successful people seem to have.

how do you build that? how do you begin to create self-belief when so often it seems we just doubt ourselves and doubt that our dreams actually can come true.

i happened upon a great video from tony robbins[12] about why some people take massive action and get great results, while others fail to do the same. the big difference that tony found existed between those two groups of people was that the people who take action are the ones that get themselves to a state of absolute certainty. he says that when you don't believe you can get the result you in fact *won't* get the result; and the way to create that level of certainty is to get the results in your head first... to feel absolutely certain, as though it has already happened... to condition yourself to believe.

so i gave it a go. i picked something that i was working on and i tried to visualize the big result that i was longing for with absolute certainty, like it was a done deal... as though it had already happened.

and i found i just couldn't visualize it! the moment i pictured the big result all of the doubts and worries and niggling negative thoughts would creep in. (thus proving tony's premise that i would not take massive action!)

when i talk about the idea of creating certainty with other women the thing i hear the most is "nothing is certain."

maybe that is just us letting our fear do the talking; if we don't get our hopes up, we won't crash as far down when it doesn't happen. or maybe it's just being pragmatic or realistic; nothing is a given of course, no matter how much we try to will it into being.

it seems to me that many women aren't that comfortable picturing the massive result as a certainty. it's ok to have that BIG vision, those BIG crazy dreams... but we definitely keep them in the dream camp. if they come true... awesome. if not... well, it was just a dream... a 'pipe' dream perhaps.

it's funny... nobody seems to mind if you have big dreams for yourself... just as long as you don't do anything too crazy, like believe in it so deeply that you take massive action that will ensure those dreams come true!

so here is a little trick i found to help build certainty without freaking myself out trying to picture such a BIG result that it triggers all my fear and i give up before i even get started.

i sneak up on that big result and build the certainty slowly.

i start with *what i know for sure.* (thank you to oprah winfrey[13] for planting that wonderful phrase in my head!)

so let's try it out with this book as an example. i could try to picture a massive result: *new york times best seller! yah baby!* but i know myself... i know that would just trigger all sorts of 'who am i to write a book?' 'who am i to talk about this stuff?' 'who am i too help people with their life journey?' bullshit thoughts. i wouldn't even be able to start the book with all of that going on in my head!

so i start with *what i know for sure* and i build up from there.

i know for sure that i have stories to tell. i know for sure that i love to write. i know for sure that when i write i make sense of the world around me. i know that sharing stories is healing and empowering and liberating. i know that when i write i make things click (for myself and for others too.) i know for sure that when i talk about the lighthouse it resonates. i know for sure that many women are struggling with the same things i am. i know that life is better when we don't feel alone, when we know someone else is cheering us on, when we feel like we have tools in our toolbelt to build the life we want for ourselves. i know for sure that i already have an audience of women who are waiting to learn more. i know for sure that sharing lessons from the lighthouse has made a huge difference to quite a few people already. i know for sure that writing this book will make a huge difference to ME.

and so i write. i take massive action... i write every day for a month until the book is all down on the page. and then i do what it takes to edit it and publish it. because i have already made it this far, i will keep going. and i take one little step at a time, one day at a time, because anything else feels overwhelming.

for me, taking massive action doesn't need to mean a massive amount of work, a massive to do list, or massive overwhelm! it means you wake up every morning and you do one thing towards that goal. and you do it again and again.

building absolute certainty is easier when you start with something that is already absolutely certain, and then you take little jumps from there.

what do you know for sure?

start with that. be committed to it. decide: *this is what i am doing. this is my vision.* and then do what it takes to get there.

you need to back yourself... be the fierce warrior that fights for what you know for sure.

belief

i am an over-achiever slash perfectionist. growing up, i was the 'smart one.'

the first time i realized i was the smart one i was in grade five and i won an award for having the top marks of my year level. before that, i knew i was smart, but that moment is when i officially became 'the smart one' in my mind and also officially got addicted to achieving top marks. yep...

my name is karen and i am addicted to A+'s

even when i started my career as a teacher i was still getting a report card of sorts - we received yearly evaluations and had to meet with our principal, grade leader, and subject leaders to be evaluated.

even as a teacher i still wanted to receive A+'s.

growing up and through my career i learned what i needed to do to be the top of my class. and i happily did it.

but the trouble is, once i was a business owner no one was giving me a report card any more. i have no boss or team leader or project manager or principal evaluating me, giving me gold stars or A+'s or report cards.

instead we business owners have clients, customers, fans, and communities.

what i find interesting is that everything we do, we do for them.

we aim to be of service. we aim to solve problems. we aim to connect with them.

but when they tell us that they love us, how deeply do we believe them?

and i think this would be the same for many of us in our everyday lives, doing the work that lights us up - as employees, as volunteers, as partners, as mothers, as community members, and as individuals.

what is your response when someone tells you they absolutely adore what you do?

do you brush it off? *"oh, it's nothing..."*

do you change the subject?

do you say thank you but then promptly dismiss it in your mind?

do you feel uncomfortable or unworthy or embar-
rassed?

do you chalk it up to luck, or people just being nice?

it's funny isn't it?

it's like praise coming from a boss is great, but
praise coming from a customer or a friend or a
stranger feels like 'they are just being nice.'

(and then deep down we wonder... what if i'm not
really doing a good enough job?)

but think about it: if *you* took the time to email
someone to tell them why you love what they do,
that wouldn't be 'just being nice' - that would be
genuine, heartfelt praise, wouldn't it?

when someone tells you they love what you do,
believe them!

it's ok to accept praise.

it's ok to believe the praise.

it's ok to be proud of the praise.

it's ok to tell the world that you are proud of the
praise.

it's ok to agree with the praise.

it's ok to feel worthy of the praise.

it's ok to own that praise - to let it become another layer of confidence and worthiness and belief.

the next time someone tells you that you are awesome, please try one of the following:

screen cap it and share it; create a shareable image with that feedback and share it; print it out and put it on your wall beside your workspace and read it daily; ring up your bestie or your hubby and say "guess what i just heard!" and celebrate it.

in other words... don't just say "oh, thanks" and then push it aside... say "thanks" and then OWN IT.

let it sink in. let it become part of your strong foundation. believe in your own brilliance!

focus

i volunteer at my daughters' school and at a recent meeting the leadership staff were sharing with us parents the work they are doing with our kids in regards to fostering a growth mindset.

so many of our students fall into a fixed mindset - they are certain of failure, even before they allow themselves give it a go.

> i can't do it.

> i don't know enough.

i am not ready.

it isn't good enough.

it's not working.

the teachers shared some examples of what this feels like to a child and how we can foster a growth mindset instead... one where our kids embrace challenges, persist even in the face of obstacles, and are inspired by the success of others.

we watched a fantastic ted talk by carol dweck called *the power of believing you can improve*[14] where the big take away message was the concept of 'yet' and how it can be a very effective way to shift your mindset.

i can't do it, yet.

i don't know enough, yet.

i am not ready, yet.

it isn't good enough, yet.

it's not working, yet.

see how that one word changes everything?

as we talked about encouraging a growth mindset in our children i had another one of those 'ah ha' moments.

those fixed 'go to thoughts' that plague our kids are the very same ones i hear from the women i work with. and what a powerful piece of knowledge that is!

when we work on our own mindsets - when we build our foundation and build ourselves - just think of what we are teaching our children by example.

damn that excites me.

so many times we feel guilty when we work on ourselves... when we work to find our purpose and live a life that ignites us. we need to start flipping our thinking about that, and realize that when we build ourselves it is actually a huge gift to those around us.

the children in our lives learn by watching us, they learn by modelling us, they are influenced by us more so than any other people in their lives. who are we NOT to teach our children that it pays to persevere, that we can learn anything we set our minds to, that we can challenge ourselves, that our effort and attitude determine everything!

one of my favourite mantras is this: what we focus on expands.

if we focus on the fact that we can't do it, we aren't good enough, and it won't work... guess what happens?

as mike dooley[15] wonderfully reminds us: *thoughts become things.*

that stuff we are hanging onto so tightly, obsessing over, insisting on... that ends up being where we invest all of our energy. it's like we are trying to prove that we are right. and so of course we manifest that exact reality for ourselves.

for instance, when we focus on all of the ways in which we are not good enough, we only see the evidence that proves us to be right: "see, i told you i wasn't good enough!"

instead we ought to focus on what we want *more* of in our lives, who we truly want to *be*, and how we really want to feel.

what we focus on becomes reality - choose wisely!

take action

there is one mantra that i probably repeat most often - to myself and to the women i talk with every day - which was inspired by seth godin's blog post on tattoo thinking.[16]

it's not a tattoo.

all of the stuff you have been and done and thought and said up until right now? it's not a tattoo.

you can change. you can stop. you can start.

all that stuff you are longing to do and explore and try and discuss and BE? it's not a tattoo either.

you can try it, test it, have some fun with it, tweak it... experiment a little. put yourself out there in all of your complete imperfection. and as you learn more, and do more, and experience more... you can keep changing!

because it's not a tattoo.

in fact you are supposed to learn and grow and evolve and tweak and play and explore. you are *not* supposed to stay permanently stuck. whatever has you stuck right now, whatever place you are in that feels like YUCK, that's also not a tattoo. that does not have to be your forever thing. you can choose differently. you can do differently.

the very first book i ever wrote was an ebook about branding, which i sold as a PDF from my website years ago. i have not looked at that book in a very long time but i am sure if i did right now i would probably think it is complete crap: because i know so much more now about that topic, because i am likely a much better writer now, and because that ebook probably did not have enough of my own personality in there.

but i do not regret that ebook even for one moment. i had to take that step in order to get to where i am today.

the same is true of the very first photo i ever took for my photography business - that photo is not all that great in hindsight but it was the first thing i ever sold as a business owner and it was an amazing first step.

please, allow yourself to be imperfect, on purpose.

where aren't you taking action? is there something you know you want to do or *need* to do, are even excited about doing, but you are still NOT doing it?

do that thing now, while it is NOT perfect, NOT ready, NOT professional, NOT enough. do it anyways, on purpose!

have the intent of taking a first step. of learning and adjusting and making it better as you go.

because when you wait for everything to be perfect first, you will resist making changes afterwards, even if you know deep down the changes are needed.

plus, we learn by doing. we get clarity by doing. we see what works and what doesn't, and then we can make things better. we can make and see progress!

and it even makes it fun to be imperfect - knowing that is actually the goal here.

so just take action in some way. take one step. and then figure out the next step.

please, give yourself permission today.

start. or stop. or make a change. put it out there. try. explore.

because it's not a tattoo.

hey, you might even want to tattoo that somewhere so you can remember it! or at least print it out and post it somewhere visible.

and the next time that voice in your head says, "you can't." answer: "who says? it's not a tattoo!"

rituals

we already have many rituals in our lives. we have things we do every morning when we wake up, every night before bed, every time we sit down to work, every time we finish up our work for the day. but are these rituals serving you?

we must create new rituals - ones that will help us to build those qualities that will help us make our dreams a reality - such as: certainty, worthiness, confidence, self-belief, resilience, gratitude, positive thinking, an abundance mindset, commitment, etc.

what new ritual would help you to build a stronger foundation for your lighthouse?

i love using the word ritual, by the way (instead of routine or schedule or even daily practice)... it feels sacred, more special, more purposeful. something you would *choose* to do instead of *have* to do.

i remember going through a bout of feeling like i was not accomplishing much compared to other entrepreneurs in my circle who had started around the same time as i had. i got into a space of feeling really down on myself - not confident, not worthy. my foundation was cracking.

one night i found myself aimlessly scrolling through facebook before bed and came across yet another one of my peers posting in a business group celebrating a major win and i felt my confidence falter once again.

i had this moment where i could hear a voice of reason in my head say: what are you moaning about? you've accomplished so much! focus on *your* wins instead of someone else's!

i could suddenly see that i had created this ritual - this daily action of wasting time on facebook - that was keeping my mindset in a place that was not very strong (or very productive!)

it was time to create a new ritual - one that would boost my confidence and strengthen my foundation instead of depleting it! i started doing what i call the 'awesome list.' it actually started as a gratitude journal but i found that i didn't just want to list the things i was grateful for, i also wanted to list my wins and everything i wanted to celebrate, i wanted to list all of the uplifting messages i received each day, the things i've accomplished, the times i listened to my intuition... so many awesome things!

it is not always easy to create a new ritual because our existing rituals are so ingrained in our lives, and change can be hard. i find it works best to tack a new ritual onto something that you already do. if you sit down for a coffee or a cup of tea around the same time each day (which is already a ritual in and of itself), tack a new ritual onto that!

i also find it helpful to set alarms on my phone for my daily rituals and to block weekly and monthly rituals into my calendar. whether it is a ritual to plan out my week or a ritual for self-care or a ritual for my spiritual practice or a ritual to celebrate a success... it matters if you say it does. the ritual becomes sacred because we say it is so.

the key is to add foundation-building rituals into your life so that they become second nature... and try to make them fun! make it a treat or a game, make it special or luxurious or fabulous!

in recent years i have become interested in the moon cycles and how they can affect our daily lives. for my whole life i have struggled with insomnia - it's just always been something i have had to deal with (and i haven't dealt with it very well i must admit... but at least i no longer just pull all-nighters all the time, like i did in university!)

and then - in the span of one week where i was not sleeping at all - i had two different people say to me in two different conversations: "oh yes, i have the worst insomnia too. *i always do when there is a full moon.*"

what the... what?

this is a thing? why didn't i know this was a thing?

and so i started noticing. i didn't change anything in my life, i just tried to make note of when the insomnia would come and go and sure enough, i would have it for the week of the full moon (a few days before and after.)

so that's when i started to get interested in the moon cycles, and i am discovering that these are wonderful times to build rituals into your month.

at the new moon: set an intention (or dream big) for the month ahead; for the quarter moon: focus on where you need to take action; at the full moon: do a big release of everything that is no longer serving your light; and in the third quarter moon: focus on gratitude. it is a simple little ritual that takes just a moment every week but feels so positive!

rituals do not have to be elaborate or time consuming. (you don't need to burn incense or say special incantations!) they are really about bringing awareness to the moment... for asking: does this serve me? does this build me up? and if not, what can i do instead? for creating new moments and patterns that do build you up instead of keeping you stuck.

expand

in september 2011, i posted my first ever quote image on my biz blog.

(note, this was before quote images were even a thing. i was ahead of the curve in this area, but a compelling photo with an inspiring quote was the exact type of image that got me starting my photography biz, and the sort of thing i loved creating for my clients, and myself.)

i felt called to create and share this image, thinking that perhaps i could use photos and quotes to inspire other women in biz on their journey. looking back, it was one of those pivotal moments in my biz journey... one that led me to where i am now.

the image was of my then three year old daughter wearing a pink ballerina swimsuit with a pair of gumboots, along with a quote from darren criss: *"there is nothing more badass than being who you are."*[17]

my daughter, to this day, has got a really quirky sense of fashion that never fails to entertain us, and she definitely has a mind of her own. i have always let her choose her own clothes because i believe that it's not a battle worth having, plus it is a safe and harmless way for her to exert her independence and creativity.

when she was three years old she picked out this pink ballerina swimsuit while shopping, and then we could barely get it off her for the next four months. it wasn't too bad when we were in canada where it was summer, but then we arrived back in australia where it definitely was not summer yet!

she wore it everywhere: to preschool, to the shops, out for dinner, you name it. we would get a lot of looks in the shopping centre and a lot of comments from well-meaning adults about how cold she must be. and when it started looking particularly ratty i definitely got my share of judgey looks, usually from other mums or women.

but each day that came - where she would insist on wearing her beloved ballerina swimsuit - i would just admire her more and more.

to be three years old and to not give a crap what other people think of you; to wear something you love because you really love it; to completely ignore other people's comments about the cold, or the stains, or the interesting choice of accessories... well i think it is pretty freaking awesome.

at the time, i remember hoping that quality about her would never change. and it hasn't! she still chooses her clothing, hair, shoes, and accessories completely based on what she loves and she ignores what anyone else thinks about it. i love it!

i think it is pretty badass to be who you are - no apologies, no regrets. and every time i look at my crazy little girl i want to remind myself of that.

a few months ago (years after this story and quote image were originally shared) i came across a business conference happening here in australia. the website said that it was going to be *different* - unlike any other biz event you've attended. they were looking for dynamic speakers who were willing to put themselves 'out there' with a twist of silliness, frivolity, and fun.

as i was reading that, i thought: oh there is no way i can apply to be a speaker at that event. that's just not *me*.

i was about to close the website when i came to the point that asked: would you be willing to dress up in a tutu to speak on stage?

with crystal clarity, the image of my daughter in a tutu and the caption about being badass popped into my head (an image that i hadn't thought about in years.)

it was an absolute 'ah ha' moment.

i used to identify as badass.

i used to identify as bold and fearless and unapologetic.

i was the girl who would get up on the table top in the middle of the local pub to sing along with whatever fun song came on the speaker.

i was vocal, opinionated, and passionate about all sorts of issues... i was the girl you didn't mess with because i didn't put up with shit, from anyone, ever.

i was the newbie blogger who said: nope i am not using capitals and i really don't care if you don't like it because i am being me... no apologies.

what happened to that girl?

what happened to feeling badass?

that was such an important 'ah ha' moment for me - reminding me that every single day i still need to (symbolically) pull on my big girl tutu and a funky pair of gumboots and boldly march out onto centre stage.

i've decided that badassery must move along a sliding scale.

the no capitals thing simply felt like *me* at that particular stage and i didn't think anything of it. (no one was going to read my blog so it didn't matter! i could just be me!) and then when i did get readers, ones who either loved or loathed the no caps, it felt pretty badass to be me and not give a fuck what anyone else thought of it. (unless of course they loved it, then i felt totally badass for being so badass.)

and then after a while, that just felt normal again. what was once badass became everyday life.

i believe that we need to keep expanding into whatever new levels are waiting for us next... remembering what that feeling of absolute badassery feels like and striving to feel it again in new ways.

and this is true of all the elements of our mindset... we need to keep expanding outwards, nudging ourselves out of our comfort zone, reaching for new levels of confidence and strength.

each new level of success we reach in our lives will require new foundation blocks to support it. keep expanding.

worthiness

when i first started thinking about the lighthouse as something that might possibly inspire others as well, i kept resisting talking about it.

there were so many people out there already sharing inspiring messages about purpose, authenticity, and mindset. it seemed like everyone was already saying the same thing as i wanted to say and the bullshit story that kept playing in my head about my message was:

this is not special enough.

i was telling myself that i had to wait until i had a message that was unique and different and special.

but what i was really thinking deep down was that i was not special enough to be sharing this message.

a couple of years ago i had the great pleasure of hearing lisa messenger speak at a conference. in her talk (and in her book daring and disruptive[18]) she shared many stories of pitching ideas to some major players in her industry and having some amazing opportunities in her life to meet with highly influential people.

what she learned from each of those moments and shared with us was this: we are all equal.

there was nothing more or less special about any of the people she had met with in her life, just as there was nothing more or less special about any of us in that room. we are all the same. we are all equal. we are each deserving. and we can each go after any opportunity we like. we can each share any message that matters to us.

i had been in this pursuit to feel like i was special. i was waiting for my message to feel special. but what i really needed to feel was *worthy*. enough.

when we put others on a pedestal of being 'special' or more than us in some way - just as when we put ourselves on a pedestal against others and feel that we are more than them - we create a really dangerous situation where our worthiness depends on others.

the reality is that our worthiness does not depend on anyone but ourselves. no one can come along and make us feel worthy. and no one can take our worthiness away from us.

we are all worthy. we are all deserving. we are all special. and yet no one is special... we are all the same.

we just need to start believing it!

one way that we can build our own worthiness is to celebrate our successes. we must focus on our own successes, rather than where everyone else sits on this crazy, pedestalled, 'special' scale we've created in our minds.

i believe that when we celebrate our success we anchor the feeling into our mind that we are *deserving* of the success. we remember and honour that we are indeed valuable and when we believe that of ourselves, others will believe it of us too.

earlier in this book i encouraged you to choose carefully how you follow the words *i am...* i think it is important to add now that this is not an exercise in creating money or fame or glory. it's not about being special.

it's about *meaning*. how you see yourself and define yourself is about owning your light... it's about embodying your light, and standing tall in strength from that space. just as everyone else has a right to do.

we don't need to hustle for our worthiness by making ourselves special. and we don't need to dim our light so that others who are more worthy may shine instead.

what we need to do is claim our worthiness. we need to honour ourselves and love ourselves and value ourselves and believe that we are absolutely enough just as we are.

if we want others to think we are worthy, valuable, deserving, and enough, we must first think those things of our self.

abundance

last year i had one of the most awesome experiences of my life.

i have been a fan of the TV show *supernatural* for ten years (when i say *a fan* what i actually mean is *kind of obsessed*).

a few years ago my best friend randomly met and became good friends with one of the stars of the show. (my bestie is not a fan... has never watched the show. he thinks my obsession is "weird but cute.") every time i go visit canada we joke about how bestie has to hook me up with 'the boys' (as we *supernatural* fans call the two stars of the show) but the timing has never really worked out.

leading up to my visit last summer i kept thinking about how awesome it really would be to meet the boys or visit the set or even just receive an auto- graph via my friend. i did not ask bestie for any of this, i didn't make any plans. i just kept imagining it happening in my mind, in all sorts of scenarios.

what i really kept thinking about was how freaking exciting it would be. i would imagine how much FUN it would be to see my favourite show be filmed. i imagined how excited i would be to meet them - how i would try not to act like a total dork and embarrass myself in the midst of my enthusiasm. i could picture how grateful i would be to my bestie for arranging the opportunity.

anyhow, the whole visit in canada passed by quickly and before i knew it it was nearly time to head back to australia. i made plans to be in vancouver for a few days before flying out, including plans to hang out with bestie one more time before flying off for another year.

bestie and i went back and forth a bit trying to sort out plans - we both had kids that needed babysit- ting, and i had to find my way through vancouver rush hour to get to him, but eventually we were on our way for our little date.

as he drove us to go for dinner and drinks i was babbling on as i always do, trying to fit as much into one visit as possible. i wondered where the heck we were going - we seemed to be in a residential area, which was an odd spot for a bar! - and i wondered what was up with the dudes in bright orange vests and walkie talkies lining the streets.

then he pulled into a random school parking lot and i KNEW where we were! we were at a location set for *supernatural* - they were filming right near his house and he had made arrangements with his friend, the star of the show, to bring me around to meet them and watch them film. and he had set it all up as a surprise!

i got to meet and hug and have a photograph with both stars of the show! i got to watch them film a scene! i got to sit in the iconic '67 chevy impala that is a major part of the show! i got to chat with the boys about the show and they were so NICE and welcoming and awesome!

i was just as excited and grateful and nervous and awed and delighted as i had imagined i would be. it was an hour that i will never, ever forget.

after the location set visit, bestie and i went out for dinner and drinks and he humoured me beautifully, letting me go on and on about how awesome the surprise was and how awesome he was as a friend and how awesome the boys were to have me as their special guest.

after such an amazing night, we hugged goodbye, and i hopped in my car to drive back downtown... still feeling like i needed to pinch myself to remind myself it wasn't all just a dream.

i smiled as i drove away, and flipped on the radio just as a commercial ad was ending. the very next song to come on the radio was a song called *carry on my wayward son*, by kansas - the unofficial theme song to *supernatural* fans, everywhere.

when this song came on the radio i just burst out laughing. as i will mention again later, i get little intuitive messages from songs and music all of the time... and i just *knew* this was one of those times. it was not a coincidence. i felt like it was a little message from the universe: see karen? see what you did there? you manifested this whole thing!

of course, bestie was the one to arrange it - i never asked him to do so, as i never felt that was appropriate. but i may have just quietly mentioned that if he was ever going to visit the set i could be at his front door within hours to come along - so he certainly knew what i was wishing for!

and looking back on how it all came to be... i was in the right place, spending a few days in the city where they film the show. and i had my mom along with me to babysit, so i could go on a date with bestie and see other friends and family kid-free while i was in town. plus i had spent quite a lot of time focusing not on *how* everything might happen (because i in fact had no plan to focus on), but instead on how it would *feel* if it did.

if i had just sat at home in australia wishing for all of that to happen it never would have! instead, i was in the right place at the right time, open to anything.

that song coming on the radio was a clear message to me: remember how this moment feels. remember what it feels like when a dream comes true. remember what it feels like to be showered with such amazing abundance and good fortune.

that is a fucking powerful feeling.

and it's one i try to remember and come back to often - when i am feeling like it's all just too hard, when i feel dejected because things haven't worked out, when i feel like i've lost my way... i go back to that night, to that moment.

i have the power to make my dreams come true.

i am deserving and ready and open to absolute abundance.

i simply need to focus on that BIG vision i have for myself. i have to let go of planning the hows and whens and wheres and trust that the universe will take care of all of that. i have to elevate my thoughts and emotions and focus on how amazing it will FEEL when it becomes reality. and i have to believe in the possibility of my dreams.

and then i have to show up. keep building my lighthouse. keep shining my light. because that's my job here.

and so that is what i will do.

head + heart

i spend quite a lot of time in my head. as i have mentioned, i am constantly trying to put the pieces of the puzzle together and make sense of the world around me (that is my zone of genius actually.)

my brain is always asking the questions: but why? but how?

i spend a lot of time figuring stuff out.

and that natural tendency to be in my head has certainly served me well - it is what has allowed me to be a great teacher for instance - i am able to figure things out and then make it all click for others.

but i have also learned that it's not quite enough for achieving success. there is more to the story than logic and smarts and brains and figuring.

as i've been going on this journey to learn what it means to build a lighthouse, i've had to learn how to get out of my head and into my heart.

the first time i heard that phrase i was quite frustrated actually!

what do you mean, get out of my head? i don't know how to do that? how does someone get into their heart? why? who says?

see, that's how my brain works... automatically questioning and figuring!

and you know i am the first one to say: do it *your way*. i am a thinker, a learner, a teacher... that is just what comes naturally to me.

but i also recognize that i am on this journey to grow as a person, to evolve, and to challenge myself. and i can understand that there is a duality to everything - that spending all of my time in my head may not serve me, just as it wouldn't if i spent all of my time in my heart either.

what does it mean for me to get into my heart?

feeling.

without agenda, without shame. just feel. and experience whatever it is i am going through (instead of needing to figure it out right away and find the solution or rush on to the next thing.)

dreaming.

just for the sake of dreaming. no judgement or holding back, no worries about the hows and whys and whens and wheres. just dreaming of my future self and how it will feel to be on the other side of the harbour.

sharing.

being real. being open. being raw. being emotional. allowing myself to be vulnerable and share freely. again not overthinking things, but just simply speaking my truth. (i think tapping into vulnerability is a great way to tap into your heart.)

connecting.

spending time connecting with myself in stillness and peace, with love and joy and curiosity and playfulness. what is my soul telling me? what is my intuition telling me? what is my gut instinct telling me? hmmmm... i wonder...

surrender.

again, there is a piece of me that wants to figure out what surrender is and how it's done, which is the opposite of surrender. now, when i catch myself in my head too much i will say out loud: that's it. i'm done. i surrender. i am not here to figure this out. i am here to just BE.

the tricky thing about hearts is that they ARE vulnerable. over the years i think that we build up lots of protective layers and walls to keep our hearts safe. heartbreak happens in so many little ways, in tiny moments.

when someone tells you: you are *just* a teacher, for instance. when someone tells you that you are too emotional, too sensitive, too woo-woo (or *too anything*, for that matter.) when someone makes you feel like a loser for wearing your heart on your sleeve.

we learn in those moments to get out of our hearts and into our heads. we learn to protect our hearts from those hurts... that it is much safer to stick with logic and planning and thinking (instead of feeling and allowing and sharing and dreaming.)

so perhaps part of our journey is not even so much about who we are here to become... rather it's unlearning all of that stuff that took us away from who we were.

to get out of our heads and back to our hearts.

to learn once again what it feels like to listen to our heart and go with our heart and trust our heart.

strengthening our foundation means building ourselves up and backing ourselves so that we may actually show up and shine... so that we may have something solid to support us as we do the work we are here to do.

use the spiral staircase.

it's your journey.

step towards your light.

clear your resistance.

spiral with your stuff.

keep marching on.

rise above.

honour your light.

part 5

use the spiral staircase

the spiral staircase of the lighthouse is a beautiful reminder that you are simply on a journey.

picture yourself standing inside the lighthouse, looking up at the top to where you want to be. if there were a direct ladder straight to the top, it would be freaking hard work to climb it! there is a reason they put a circular staircase inside the lighthouse... it is much easier to take one tiny little step at a time.

and even though, as you are climbing those steps, it may seem like you are going round and round and not getting anywhere... you *are* indeed. every step is taking you closer to the top of the lighthouse... to your goal, your dream, your BIG vision.

if you picture that staircase from above it is a beautiful spiral. when you look at it that way, each step is taking you closer to the centre as well. to your core. to who you are in this world and the work you are meant to be doing... to your light that you are meant to shine.

when you think about it that way, it's actually quite profound this work that we are doing here!

with each step you take, the next steps appear.

every little step you take takes you closer to the top AND to your centre.

you aren't going around in circles. it's a spiral. made of tiny little steps.

so just keep marching on. keep climbing.

the spiral staircase is about feeling empowered; it's about elevation... rising up and rising above. and it's about honouring your journey.

you are exactly where you are meant to be.

awareness

there are lots of blocks that can potentially hold you back from standing tall and owning your light. and each of us will have a completely different block from the next person. that is what makes it so hard - we each have our own 'stuff,' so there is no magic formula to work through it all.

for instance you might be blocked by:

> fearing judgement: "who is she to...?"

upsetting the status quo.

outshining others.

being seen as selfish: "it's all about me."

feeling not good enough yet.

thinking everything has already been said... it's not different or special.

worrying that when you speak up, bad things happen.

assuming no one will care.

and those are just a few of the things that could make you feel like you just can't do this! i'm sure there are many, many more!

what do you do when you are feeling blocked?

i think the most important thing is to recognize that you do have some sort of block or some kind of resistance... to see it for what it is, something that is in the way of you taking the next step of your journey.

when i notice that i have a block, i actually feel like there is a physical wall in front of me preventing me from moving forward.

for instance, i *know* i should just reply to that email and say: "yes! i would love to write a blog post for your audience, spreading my message far and wide and connecting with more of my right people! yay! sign me up!" but i just can't seem to do it! i procrastinate, i come up with excuses, i 'forget' to do it.

another sign that i have a block is when i get really triggered or annoyed by stuff i see other people doing.

for instance, if i am thinking: "who is she to be sharing that message? she's a nobody!" or "jeeze, she really goes on and on doesn't she? it's 'all about me' all the freaking time!"

those triggers are often big clues to the blocks that i might have... resistance that i might be experiencing myself.

plus, any time my response to an idea or strategy is 'but...' that is a big clue for me to pay attention to as well.

for instance, if someone says: "you should submit an article to huffington post!" and my reply sounds like: "i would, *but* someone else talked about the same thing last month." or "great idea, *but* i'm worried it would upset people in our industry." BUT is always a clue!

the first step is awareness. we've really got to open our eyes to what is going on with us, what it is deep down that is at the core of why we are feeling stuck.

i find that journaling really helps - writing down all of the buts, triggers, and avoidance; working through where they came from and exploring why they are coming up now (maybe something happened in my past that is causing this thought or belief).

sometimes it takes the help of others too. working with a mastermind group, a coach, a mentor, or a therapist can be really helpful - someone with an outside perspective and some great practical tools that can help you recognize your blocks and clear them.

i've also been trying out methods like kinesiology, reiki, and emotional freedom technique (EFT or tapping) to help shift the energy and release the blocks that seem very persistent and hard to move past! i am sure there are other techniques as well - ask around and try things out. see what people and tools come into your life and see what works for you!

the bottom line is that you have to take some sort of action: decide not to let that stuff stand in your way and then do whatever works for you!

you've got to JFDI!

this is another of my favourite mantras: *just fucking do it!* sometimes we need to give ourselves a little mental push to take action... a little symbolic slap on the ass so to speak. come on now honey, you've got this... JFDI!

i believe that overcoming these blocks is part of what we are here to do.

we are on this path because we have a purpose to find... a light to shine... but we are also here to figure out how to work through these things, so that we can grow as people and be the highest version of ourselves.

your life is a reflection of you. when you build you, you build your life! so look that block right in the eye and say, "hey, thanks for showing me what i need to work on next, i am on it!"

this is why i love the symbolism of the spiral staircase. each step is just one little step, none of them more challenging or more important than any other. if you want to rise to the top, you take the stairs!

try picturing your block as one simple step. you can either choose to stay there stuck on that one step - never moving forward, never getting any closer to the light - or you can choose to take the next step and keep going, to keep marching on.

what will you choose?

understanding

when i first started my photography business it was sort of by accident... i did it because people liked what i did and started asking how much i charge. i thought, 'why not?' and didn't really feel super invested in the outcome either way... so it didn't really trigger my fear in too big of a way. i was just happy to have something to mess around and earn a bit of spending money with.

when i started the *build a little biz* blog it was really just a little thing on the side - a place to share what i was learning about business. i thought maybe it might help someone else; and yes, there was a little voice in my head saying, "who are you to teach people about business?" but i didn't really expect anyone to even read the blog so it wasn't too hard to quiet that voice.

as time went on i've stepped up further with each phase of my business, to finding my purpose and doing work that truly lights me up, and that inner voice has gotten louder.

> who are you to help other people on their soul journey?
>
> who are you to be a thought leader, an author, a speaker?

you're probably going to fail, this is a bad idea.

you are not ready. you are not enough. you are *just* a teacher.

what i understand now, is that inner voice - or inner critic, as it is often called - is really just my ego talking; it's my lizard brain that has never really evolved and it is trying to keep me small and safe and comfy and fine.

i like to visualize a little girl when i picture that voice... a younger, more simple, less evolved version of me. sometimes she is a small, worried child pulling on my hand, pulling me away from danger. sometimes she is a tantrum-y toddler, stomping her feet and yelling, "no, i don't want to and you can't make me!" other times she is a hormonal teenager who just wants to hide in her room all day because life is just way too painful; she shouts, "no one cares anyway!" before she slams the door.

(i call my mini-me inner critic 'karen brandy,' because you know you gotta pull out both names when you are talking to the naughty child!)

the thing about children is that they don't mean to be naughty, so it reminds me not to think of her too harshly! they act based on instinct and circumstance. they are not always aware of the full story, they only see things from one point of view and they just lash out and react. it's our job, as the adult in this situation, to pull back on their hand and guide them gently and with love into a better, more helpful space.

as we know, on this journey we are here to grow and learn and evolve. it's simply what we are here to do. so as we step closer into our purpose, closer to our light, that danger and pain and frustration feels bigger than ever. because now this is personal! this isn't something that doesn't matter if we fail at, this *means* something.

so our inner mini-me wants to protect us more than ever and that's why it's so useful to have one! the very thing that inner voice wants to hold us back from the most, is often the very thing we are here to do.

we can learn a lot from our fear as well, for the same reason.

of course, fear can absolutely keep us safe - when we have that fear reaction in our gut we should definitely note it! for instance, if you are about to get in an elevator with a strange dude, trust your gut on that!

the trouble is that fear doesn't distinguish between all of the types of 'not safe' in your life. the fear reaction to when we are about to start writing a new book, for instance, or when we are about to talk to a new group of people about what we care about the most... that fear is not all that helpful if it gets in the way of us shining our light.

how can you tell the difference?

listen to your body... your body knows.

i can often feel a sensation like a physical pull-back when my inner critic voice is trying to take over... like she is pulling on my hand away from the danger. that sensation is how i know it's my mini-me doing the talking and she is not actually the one that is meant to be the boss here... i am.

so i will say: "hey, karen brandy, thanks for trying to keep me small and safe and comfy, but it's ok, i've got this." and instead of letting her pull my hand away, i will take hers and move us both along.

part of our job here is to learn and explore and understand what is really going on with us - what is blocking our next step, what is pulling back on our hand to keep us from taking the next step.

the more we understand the easier it is to actually do something about it all!

illumination

how do you move past the fear, the doubt, the worry, and everything else that is holding us back?

when we shine a light on the darkness it loses its power.

fear, doubt, and worry build and grow and fester in the darkness. and most of us tuck that stuff away in the dark, because it's so much easier to do that than it is to push through it all. but safe and small and comfy is actually a pretty unsatisfying way to live.

often times just being aware of what is happening is enough... being aware that the inner voice exists, being aware of the fears and how they are holding us back, being aware that it is all simply part of this journey and what we are here to deal with.

shine a light on it. *i see you there, and i don't care. i'm going to keep going.*

the other thing i like to try is to let it all play out in my mind's eye... instead of hiding in the dark, actually follow the fear and see where it takes you.

what is the biggest fear you have?

as i thought about writing this book, my biggest fear was that it would be absolutely terrible. i wasn't afraid that other people would read it and hate it, i was afraid that i would put my entire heart and soul and story and passion down on the page and then *i* would read through it and realize it was all just a steaming heap of shit.

that thought still makes my heart pound even as i type it.

because i think that would be rather heart break-ing... to be excited about a project, to be absolutely inspired and committed and ready, and to put all of the time and energy into it, only to read it all back and find out it is actually shit.

i wouldn't care that much if other people didn't like it, but i would be crushed if i put all of that love into it and *i* didn't like it! i would feel like i let myself down, and i would feel like i didn't do this idea justice. that maybe i wasn't cut out to be an author, a spiritual teacher, a soulful leader in this space of inspiring and transforming women.

and then what would i do? what would i be left with?

that's what really scares me.

so that is where you want to let your fear out to play... what would i actually do if that worst fear happened?

i thought about it, and i guessed that i would not give up. i would work on the book until it was no longer a pile of crap and make it better. maybe i would hire an editor to help me. maybe i would re-organize my thoughts and start again. maybe i would need to do some self-work to build up my confidence and belief again.

but i wouldn't give up. i wouldn't quit.

the alternative is just not an option. giving up on this dream i have, going back to a desk job, working to help someone else create their dream... i just can't comprehend that. and just because the book sucks, doesn't mean the whole dream - the whole lighthouse revolution - should be trashed.

so i know that even if this book is a flop, i will keep going... it will be just another step on this journey.

and suddenly that fear doesn't hold much power over me anymore.

but what if that fear does end up coming true? well my plan is to yell BINGO and pat myself on the back for having called it.

truly, you have got to try that! think about any situation that is causing you some stress, write down what you are afraid of happening, and predict what is totally going to trigger you... what is going to make you feel stuck. and then when it happens shout BINGO (even if you shout it in your head). it totally turns the situation around - suddenly that horrible thing is now kind of silly, and really... you've got this!

(a little update: so i am reading this section of the book again a few months later, and i totally had forgotten that this was my big fear! as soon as i wrote this story down - shone a light on my fear and let it all play out and realized that even if the fear comes true i would still be ok - it did indeed lose its power! i wanted to add this comment here now to share that though i know this strategy works, it still surprised me that it worked! ha! so do try to shine a light on your fear - you just might be surprised too!)

reflecting

one of the most important lessons i have been reminded of on my own journey to live my purpose is this: my stuff is the only stuff i can work on.

it seems obvious, but how many times do we say things like: he made me feel like a loser; she is not giving me any support; he is so critical of everything i do; she is just so negative about everything!

and all of that may very well be true, i am not saying that any one of us is not entitled to feel any of these things. but in the end, what can we really do about it?

we can't change other people, we can't control other people, we can't force other people to work on their stuff. the only thing we can do is work on our own stuff.

one of the best tools i have learned on this journey is to hold up a mirror... simply imagine holding up and looking into a mirror in your mind's eye.

doing this helps me to recognize that their stuff is indeed their stuff and i let all of that bounce back to them... i can't control it or change it.

and what i see when i look in that mirror is me... it's my stuff.

if i am letting a situation get to me, if i just can't let it go and move on, it's a sign that there is something there that i need to work on.

i often use this trick of holding up a mirror when i find myself really angry with someone, really hurt by something someone said, not able to let go of something (even when i recognize that what they have said or done is more about them than it is about me), feeling really triggered by a person or a comment, or simply feeling really annoyed by a situation.

i catch myself and say: "whoa, maybe it's time to hold up the mirror. what is going on here? what is being reflected back at me in this situation? what am i here to learn?"

here are some ideas for you:

> what i feel i am not getting from others is a reflection of what i am not giving myself.

> the pain i experience in an interaction with another person is a reflection of a wound i need to heal in myself.

> the criticism that bothers me from others is a reflection of the criticism i am already giving myself... that inner voice in my head.

> the relationships i have with others are a reflection of the relationship i have with myself.

> the phrase, "she made me feel like..." is a reflection of how i already feel about myself deep down inside.

> my financial worth is a reflection of my self-worth.

> the anger i feel towards others is a reflection of the anger i am directing to myself.

> how i am wanting to make someone else feel, by expressing my anger, is a reflection of how they made me feel (and what is really triggering me here.)

the mirror also works when you are wanting to achieve something. try reflecting what you want most back onto others...

> if you want to feel included... include.

> if you want to be invited... invite others in.

> if you want engagement... engage.

> if you want to feel loved... give yourself love first.

> if you want to feel valued... value others, and show them that you value yourself.

the only person or situation you can control is yourself!

the life that you are building for yourself is a reflection of you... of your energy, of your soul's journey, of your own self-love.

so if you find that you are stuck with something in your life - in your work, in your relationships, or wherever - hold up the mirror and ask yourself:

how is this a reflection of my 'stuff?'

let's say in your work you find that you've hit a plateau... a ceiling... where you don't feel like you are taking your career or your business to the next level.

how can you push yourself personally to the next level? how can you shake things up in your own soul journey, or spiritual journey, or your self-healing, or whatever?

let's say in your relationships you feel like you aren't getting what you need, you feel frustrated or annoyed all of the time.

how can you give yourself more of what you need? how can you love and honour and respect yourself first, above any other relationship?

let's say as you beam your light and share YOU with the world, you feel like no one even notices you, you feel like you aren't being seen or heard or very impactful.

how are you not listening to yourself? how are you hiding yourself in some way. how are you not seeing yourself clearly?

when you start thinking like a mirror, your perspective on the stuff that gets you stuck will begin to change.

i've found that i am more quickly able to see most situations as opportunities for me to grow and to learn (rather than automatically going to the state of moaning, blaming, and complaining.)

i don't always see what the mirror is telling me right away - some of this stuff is hard to learn about ourselves. but awareness is always the first step.

reframing

related to the idea of mirrors and reflections, is developing the ability to flip things around in your head, to reframe your thoughts and turn negative emotions into positive ones.

this is especially useful if you see what someone else is doing and think: why can't that be me? why can't i have that life? why is she so lucky? why didn't i do that first? why why why?

in other words, you go straight to comparison, jealousy, thinking you are too late, thinking you are not enough.

this is a moment to catch yourself and flip your thinking by remembering this: the light you see in others is a reflection of the light that is in you.

what you are jealous of in others is often a sign of what it is you really want for yourself. go back to your BIG vision and add that in!

when you are annoyed because someone else is doing the exact same thing you were thinking of doing, see it as a sign that you are on the right track, and that it is needed.

when you are envious of someone else's success, it's a reminder to you that it is possible, it is achievable, and it's your turn next.

if you let them, these moments can easily turn into the crappy stuff that gets you stuck on your journey or makes you want to give up.

or you can recognize that this is another one of those mirror moments and choose to know instead that the light you see in others is a reflection of the light that you are here to shine.

when i wrote my first blog post about the lighthouse revolution i had such a wonderful response from readers that i felt absolutely certain that i was on to something special.

and then, within 24 hours, i started seeing lighthouses everywhere. i opened up a book by one of my favourite authors and spiritual leaders - lighthouse. i popped onto instagram and saw a post from a massively successful business coach - lighthouse. i was searching for something on google and came across a book about business and marketing - yep, another lighthouse.

i had a moment of absolute dejection. i couldn't have a lighthouse revolution - a brand new way of thinking about the life we are here to build - if other people were already talking about lighthouses! it wouldn't be a revolution!

and then i took a deep breath and thought: if this were someone i was helping, what would i tell them? what would the lighthouse teach us in this situation?

the light you see in others is a sign.

i pictured the universe sending me a message: *see karen, you are on the right track. you wanted lighthouses so we sent you lighthouses. keep going!*

and so instead of quitting before i had barely started, i decided that i would take it as a sign that now it's *my time* to shine my light, and these other people are here to help me.

in fact, whenever i come across people who are talking about the same thing that i am, i try to see them as torch bearers who are walking beside me on this journey. i say to myself: wow, this hugely famous author is helping me to share my message and shine a light on this! how awesome is that!

a very similar thing happened as i was about to start writing this book. a friend gave me a newly released book that was pretty popular in the spiritual/transformational space. it was a great book, i loved it, but as i was reading it i had a tiny moment of panic where i thought: *this is basically what i want to say with my book! gah!*

then i stopped that thought right in its track. i needed to flip my thinking... i needed to see this situation as a mirror.

the universe sent that book my way - via this friend - so i thought: *what would you have me learn here?* i kept reading and for every chapter i thought: *yep i knew that, yep i figured that out already, yep that was a big ah ha moment for me too.*

and then it came to me - that book was a mirror to show me that i was READY. i know my stuff, i know exactly what helps, i know how to tell this story... it's time to write *my* book.

i just love having an 'ah ha' moment like that! in that moment i had two choices: i could stay in a downward spiral of comparison, dejection, and misery (and give up on my book altogether) or i could choose to flip the situation around and look for a positive spin on it... i could choose the upward spiral.

in the end it is our choice... try to reframe things and rise above!

there is one more way i have found that flipping my thinking can help. if i am really struggling with something i try to see how i can flip that situation on its head and do the very opposite to how i feel.

if i am hanging on to my anger, i look for where i need to let go and forgive.

if i find myself complaining and focusing on the negative, i stop and say something super positive.

if i am feeling overwhelmed and mentally scattered, i will do some decluttering and clearing of my physical space.

if i find myself feeling like there is way too much to do and not enough time, i will stop and say out loud: "i have all the time in the world" and take a moment to just sit and be.

the stuff we are focusing on so intently can often be a sign of what we really need in order to move past it - we just tend to keep our focus on the same old thing when what we really need to do is the very opposite.

try to catch yourself in those moments, flip the situation around, and do the opposite of whatever it is you are stressing out about.

again, choose the upward spiral instead of the downward one.

clearing

here is the thing we need to remember as we work to ignite our own light...

we can do all of the things listed in this book - we can be ourselves and ignite our light, we can share who we are and be a beacon, we can build a life that serves our light - but if our windows are all clouded over, our light still won't shine very bright.

what clouds up our windows?

those thoughts of: who am i to...? i am not enough to... i am just a...

and all of the doubts: in your ability, your value, your worthiness...

plus all of the fears: of failure, of upsetting people, of what will happen if...

along with all of the lack: of belief, of self-worth, of certainty, of positivity.

those are all things that will cloud up your windows and prevent you from shining your light. and only you can clear them away. it's actually part of your job to clear them away.

we've already said that your light is energy. it is the high vibration energy of love, joy, peace, authenticity, inspiration, and growth. the presence of low vibration thoughts, doubts, fears and lack will just cloud up all of that energy... making your light feel very dim.

i know this whole book is about building your light-house so that you can shine, but it's not actually our job to *find* the light. our job is to clear away all of the fog, the blocks, the resistance to the light.

marianne williamson, in her book *a return to love*[19], says this so very perfectly:

"our deepest fear is not that we are inadequate. our deepest fear is that we are powerful beyond measure. it is our light, not our darkness that most frightens us. we ask ourselves, 'who am i to be brilliant, gorgeous, talented, fabulous?' actually, who are you not to be? you are a child of god. your playing small does not serve the world. there is nothing enlightened about shrinking so that other people won't feel insecure around you. we are all meant to shine, as children do. we were born to make manifest the glory of god that is within us. it's not just in some of us; it's in everyone. and as we let our own light shine, we unconsciously give other people permission to do the same. as we are liberated from our own fear, our presence automatically liberates others."

you need to become your own lighthouse keeper - the keeper of your light, the one who keeps the fuel tank full, keeps the foundation strong, keeps the tower decluttered, and yes... keeps the windows and the light reflectors crystal clear.

when i first started talking about the lighthouse revolution one of my blog readers said something very beautiful that went something like this: maybe when you are in your lighthouse you cannot see how bright your own light is.

we don't often see ourselves clearly. we don't fully realize the beautiful, amazing people we are or the gifts we have to share with the world. and we certainly don't realize how cloudy our windows are either... especially when they get that way slowly and subtly, over time, as is so often the case.

last year i was talking with one of my best friends who has an amazing gift of being able to see so clearly who people are at their core. i find this to be true especially with children; she just sees them differently, she sees and notices and is aware of so many nuances that i certainly never pick up on. it's a really beautiful quality that i admire and am often in awe of.

when i mentioned it to her, she was kind of surprised. she didn't think there was anything unique at all about how she sees people but as we chatted further we worked out that this truly is a beautiful gift and we even thought about how this might come into play in the business that she is building.

as i have mentioned before from my own experience - when someone sees you as being more than you ever thought possible, when someone cracks open the cloudy window and alters how you see yourself in the world, that is a profound moment.

as i have experienced, and as my friend did as well, this moment is often followed by weeks and months of unhelpful thoughts, fears, doubts, and lack bubbling up to the surface.

who i am to be this new version of me? how can i possibly step into and own this expanded view of myself? what will people think? i am not ready.

sometimes when this happens, we will even dim our light on purpose, keep it safe and hidden away, because it is easier to just keep being the smaller, less profound version of ourselves. but even when we keep our light hidden away, it will keep tapping us on our shoulder until we pay attention.

once you open the window, even just a crack, there is no closing it again! your light is just waiting to shine! and so you must do the work to clear away anything that is resisting, blocking, or clouding your light.

your light is energy - everything you add to your lighthouse has to be an energetic match to the beautiful energy of love, joy, peace, growth, inspiration, and authenticity that lives inside you. there is no room in your lighthouse for unhelpful thoughts, doubts, fears, or lack. clear that stuff away... it does not love your light, it does not serve you anymore.

compassion

when i was talking with my best friend about her amazing gifts i of course wanted to sweep away all of those unhelpful thoughts right out of her lighthouse, i wanted to shake them right out of her, because i know how fucking amazing she is! (and i know she has wanted to do the same to me on occasion!)

what if we treated ourselves with the same compassion that we offer to our best friends?

picture your best friend (or perhaps even your own daughter) sitting right beside you: struggling with whatever she is stuck with, feeling like she is not enough, spiralling with all of that doubt and lack and fear. what would you say to her?

would you tell her that she is absolutely enough? would you tell her all of the ways that she matters? would you let her know that the destination on the other side of the fear is so worth it?

of course you would! and yet we don't think twice about beating ourselves up over the very same things that would break our hearts to hear our best friends say about themselves.

we are often so much kinder to others than we are to ourselves, we have more compassion for others than we do ourselves.

we are also fiercely protective of our best friends and our daughters - our inner mama bear comes out to defend the people we care so much about.

we need to train ourselves to be just as kind to ourselves and just as fiercely protective of ourselves. when you catch yourself stuck in negativity, interrupt it with this phrase: would you talk to your best friend like that?

another idea is to picture a much younger version of yourself, struggling with the same things that you are beating yourself up with now: judgement, criticism, guilt, embarrassment, regret, unworthiness, dejection...

visualize a little girl with those same feelings, covering her face in shame. what would you say to her? i bet you would hug her tight, hold her close, dry her tears, and shower her with love.

we judge ourselves so harshly - and all of that shame just grows bigger with judgement.

in order to shift this stuff, in order to clear and heal and grow and move on, we need to douse all of our shame in empathy, understanding, and compassion. we need to love, honour, and cherish ourselves... just as we would do for that little girl.

we need to stop beating ourselves up and start loving ourselves up instead!

it also helps if you can share your innermost feelings with someone else, because keeping it all to yourself - in secrecy and silence - just gives it more power. just as you would remind that little girl, it really does help to share the weight with someone you trust.

as we receive compassion and understanding and empathy from others, we begin to believe we deserve it, and perhaps then we can start giving more of it to ourselves.

body wisdom

they say that fear is not so different from excitement... that the only difference is your breath. can you tell the difference? watch for it next time... begin to learn what your body is telling you.

i love this idea, because not only can both our brains and our intuition guide us, but so too can our own bodies! imagine if we could read our bodies like a book and use that knowledge to understand our journey better, to make decisions, to get unstuck!

the first type of body wisdom that i ever really picked up on was when i was feeling really stuck with something going on in my personal life.

i knew logically what i needed to do, i knew in my heart what i wanted to do, my intuition was telling me that it was time to do something to heal this situation, but i *just. could. not. do. it.*

i actually felt like there was a big brick wall blocking me from taking a step forward and doing the thing i wanted and needed to do.

no amount of logic or understanding could shift it. i knew i had to do some work on *me*, before i could take that step. i knew that i needed to clear that block, heal whatever was going on there, sweep away the stuck energy... and i did indeed go on to do all of that.

(by the way, as i have said already, how you clear your blocks is totally up to you. our world is full of all sorts of amazing techniques, practices, strategies, healers, and teachers. it's really just about finding what works for you!)

but the main thing i learned from that experience is what it feels like in my body when i've got a block that needs clearing or some issues i need to work on. if there is something energetically going on with me - something i need to shift or understand - it feels like there is a brick wall in my way. good to know!

as i've mentioned, when my inner critic is trying to protect me and keep me safe and small, it feels like someone is grabbing my hand and pulling me back so i just can't take that step forward. my head and my heart and my gut say yes but there is something there that says NO.

it's such useful body wisdom to have. i know that i am not just procrastinating or coming up with excuses or avoiding the hard jobs or whatever i used to tell myself i was doing. i know now that i've got some inner work to do before i can take any steps forward.

another body reaction that i find incredibly useful is goosebumps!

over the past two years i have been exploring my intuition more and more, and making note of what it feels like and how it happens for me. one thing i have noticed is that goosebumps are happening more often.

for me it is a sign that i have hit the nail on the head... that i'm on to something. it's like it's my body's way to get my attention and say: "hey, pay attention right now! whatever it is you are thinking about or talking about or working on... there is something in that. explore it further!"

and as for fear... as we've already mentioned, fear is there to keep you small and safe and comfy. the tricky thing is that the stuff that scares us is often the stuff we need to do on our journey.

so how do you know if the fear you are feeling is about keeping you safe from a real danger (or even just a bad idea that is going to backfire on you!) or if it is the fear that comes when you are on the edge of something really freaking awesome.

i always ask myself: does the choice feel heavy or light.

i will actually close my eyes and picture the thing i am about to do and feel it in my body - does it feel heavy? like this is just not good at all, it's going to backfire, or leave you regretting you ever said yes. or does it feel light? like your heart is racing with possibility and that any troubles you have along the way will be so worth it!

make the light choice.

we can even learn a lot from our own body language... when the choice feels light, you sit a little taller, your chest and shoulders open up. when the choice feels heavy or dark, your body slumps under the weight, you close off and get smaller in an effort to protect yourself.

your body is just one more way you can connect to your light and be aware of what is happening for you on this journey.

and so it should be! your body is the vehicle that allows you to be you and shine your light, so we should honour it and honour what we can learn from it.

forgiveness

one of the best tools for dealing with any of the stuff that comes your way is forgiveness. you can use it in all sorts of stuck situations - criticism, blame, shame, anger, frustration, humiliation, rejection, dejection - you name it. this is one strategy that i throw at everything!

the forgiveness mantra i use is a hawaiian forgiveness practice called ho'oponopono. it goes like this:

i love you. i'm sorry. please forgive me. thank you.

the way i do forgiveness is to simply picture the shit situation in my head - i might picture an interaction with another person, i might picture my younger self doing something i am still hanging onto, i might picture myself right now dealing with something sucky - and i say the mantra over and over until i feel a bit better, until i feel the energy from the situation dissolving away.

but really, it doesn't matter who or what else is involved, what you are really doing is forgiving yourself. you are clearing away whatever it is *you* perceive to be the problem, whatever is coming up for *you*. you are freeing yourself from whatever pain, shame, guilt, anger, negativity, expectations etc. you have been hanging on to so tightly.

for me, this is how it feels...

when i say *i love you*, i am saying that to myself. and imagine if we said 'i love you' to ourselves more often! that alone would be so powerful. i am also sending love - mentally, energetically - to whomever else is involved in the situation. and that is really powerful as well... it feels so much better to choose love over the darkness.

i'm sorry, is me acknowledging that this is my issue: how i am reacting, the stuff i am hanging on to... that's all mine and mine alone. i'm taking responsibility for my own stuff. and i remember that i cannot change anyone else... the only person i can change is me.

please forgive me. again i acknowledge that this is my issue; i am the one choosing to hang on to my hurt, my anger, my frustration. you might think the phrase should be 'i forgive you' (and you could always say that instead if you want to) but i actually think it is more freeing to say 'please forgive me.' it's like your brain starts to say: ok, that's enough, we aren't going to hang on to that anymore because we see that it isn't helpful and we have permission to let it go. self, you are forgiven.

and *thank you* is simply gratitude at the core. thank you for this experience, it has helped me to grow and learn. thank you for the love. thank you for the forgiveness. thank you for clearing this all away. thank you for letting this all go, so that i can move forward on this journey.

when i first learned about ho'oponopono i was very inspired and intrigued... if you want to know more about how powerful this practice is you can try joe vitale's video *healing with ho'oponopono*[20].

at that time, my hubby and i were cross with each other about some dumb thing (well it was probably dumb, as these things often are) and had one of those nights where we both went off to bed with our backs turned away from each other, our bodies perched at each edge of the mattress. good times, right? so i decided to give this ho'oponopono thing a try.

i lay there quietly, simply picturing him in my mind's eye, silently going through the mantra over and over again in my head. as i said the words i imagined sending love his way... i pictured it like a beam going from my heart to his. i began to feel my frustration and anger dissipate... i don't actually think you can say those phrases over and over and hang on to anger at the same time! i began to feel much better about whatever it was that was going on, i felt like i truly had let it all go and knew that the next day would be just fine.

and then, to my absolute surprise, my sound asleep, snoring hubby rolled over in his sleep and put his arms around me and gave me a big hug. and kept on snoring! i actually laughed out loud when that happened... what an amazing confirmation of the power of forgiveness.

somehow, not only did i clear away that crappy energy that i was hanging on to, the forgiveness practice actually changed him too (even if he didn't realize it at the time!) to this day, i try to do the forgiveness mantra every night before falling asleep... sometimes i have one thing or person or situation to think about as i do it, sometimes i just do it for myself in general. i really do think it is a powerful act of self-love.

this is just one example of a forgiveness practice, you can do whatever sort of thing suits you.

you can try writing down all of the memories that you are hanging on to, all of the stuff running through your head, all of the blocks you feel, and simply forgive each of those things one by one.

you can write it all down and burn it or wash it down the drain (that is a pretty powerful symbol of letting it all go!)

you can meditate or run it out or sit with your feet in the waves and feel it all wash away.

do whatever works for you. but do try out a forgiveness mantra like ho'oponopono - this is powerful stuff!

curiosity

as we come to the end of this chapter, it might be starting to feel like 'wow, this is a lot to deal with.' there are so many things that will come up on this journey that leave us feeling really stuck, or ready to turn back.

but please try not to see this as *hard work*. it is just part of what we are here to do.

i think that it is incredibly empowering to accept that our work here is actually to deal with all of this stuff. we are supposed to deal with it, it's why it comes up for us! it is simply part of the journey.

it is also very empowering to stop seeing this as *hard* and as *work*... to instead allow ourselves to honour this process with ease and a sense of playfulness and curiosity.

curiosity is a really powerful emotion. it sounds a bit like this: i wonder what this is really about? i wonder what i am meant to learn here? i wonder why this is coming up for me now? these phrases shift the focus away from the horrible stuckness of a situation and turn the whole thing into a simple step on the journey.

i actually think that curiosity is one of the paths to self-love; you are saying that you honour yourself enough to explore this and to learn and grow. you change the situation from beating yourself up (and maybe beating up others too!) to being curious instead, and treating yourself with love and compassion.

plus it definitely feels more empowering... i don't need to stay stuck in negative crap, i can turn it around and say "ok, what am i meant to learn from this?"

in her book *rising strong*[21], brené brown has a wonderful strategy where she says that we need to "*rumble with our story*" and i do love that (and her!), but i would actually like to shift that phrase a little to suit the whole vibe of the lighthouse revolution a bit better.

instead of rumbling - which feels an awful lot like a big fight or a wrestling match, with a winner and a loser - i think we ought to *spiral* with our story instead. to me, that feels more like a dance: we can turn the situation around and around, see it from different angles and points of view. we can rise above the block or the stuckness and see it from a different perspective, one which will allow us to both understand it and clear it.

when i spiral with my stories and stuckness i find that it helps to have a sense of wonder, of playful-ness, of exploration... it makes the process itself feel more pleasurable, more fun, instead of something that is hard work or a fight, and just completely yucky.

i actually heard someone say once that if we tack on the sound 'hmmmm...' in front of any question it activates those joyful feelings of curiosity, wonder, and play.

hmmmm... i wonder what my body is telling me right now?

hmmmm... i wonder how my intuition works?

hmmmm... i wonder if this will work to clear that block?

hmmmm... i wonder why this situation is triggering me so much?

(and doesn't that indeed feel so much more em-powering than saying: "uggggh... why the hell is this triggering me so much?")

if we feel like this 'spiral journey stuff' is all one more thing we have to do or figure out or work on, it's just going to feel stressful and constricting.

but if we come from a place of curiosity, if we find the fun in playing around and learning more about ourselves, then it opens the doors for the right stuff to come onto your path.

be curious about you. have fun learning you and spiralling with your stories. enjoy growing and evolving and developing tools that will help you deal with all of the stuck situations in your life.

i know that we each have this amazing destination that we are longing to arrive at... we do indeed want to own our light and live a life that lights us up... but remember, the journey should feel just as good as the destination will!

the journey is, after all, why we are here; so please honour it, honour yourself. allow yourself to feel whatever it is you feel, explore those feelings with curiosity and wonder, and be ready to shift anything that needs shifting.

the spiral staircase is here to remind us that we are simply on a journey and we need to honour that journey. as we take each step we must make the light choice, choose the upward spiral, and choose to elevate our thoughts, beliefs, and actions. when we find ourselves feeling stuck it is our job to explore, learn, and rise above.

find your harbour.

come home.

use your inner compass.

ride out the storms.

embrace the darkness.

be grounded.

hold on to your anchor.

come back to your light.

part 6

find your harbour

the final component of the lighthouse is the harbour... it is where your lighthouse lives.

the truth of it is, this work is not easy. it's not quick. we might falter. we might get lost once again. we might get off track and completely forget about this lighthouse we are building.

the harbour reminds us that we can come back to our lighthouse any time... we can come back inside and do a bit more work...

we can come back home.

the harbour is a safe haven for when it feels like the waves are crashing in, when we feel lost at sea, or when it feels like we are sinking.

our own lighthouse will be a beacon to us, shining a light so that we know that it's there, reminding us that everything will be all right, and pointing the way back home.

the harbour means hope. it's about coming back to you. again. and always.

the darkness

let's face it, life isn't always shiny and bright. maybe that seems contradictory for me to say, since i'm trying to convince you that you do indeed have a light to shine in this world and the best way to do that is by building a lighthouse.

but on the other side of all this awesome, shiny, beautiful light is the darkness.

and it would be really silly of us to assume that just because we decide to start shining, the darkness will suddenly stay away. and i say this from experience... i've been the silly one many times.

before i started writing this book i went through a pretty crappy period. i was angry. i was sad. i was not coping. i did not feel lit up, at all. it was all unrelated to my business, my message, this book... but it did not matter. when you are in the darkness, it ripples out to everything.

here's the thing i still had to learn from the lighthouse: when you feel ignited, when you feel lit up, when you find your spark and show up and say i am ready to shine my light... well that's awesome. it really is. there is nothing like it!

there is a reason i use the word ignited... you really do feel like someone has lit a match right under you. you feel invigorated, excited, activated! you feel like your purpose is pulling you, you feel like you are ready to bounce out of bed each day and tackle the world!

but the reality is that we just can't live like that 100% of the time. (well, i don't know... maybe some people can. i'd like to talk to those people!) i've discovered that i can't live in the light all of the time. and so many of the women i talk to have also discovered the same thing.

because we are souls in a human body, having a human experience, bound by human constraints.

the reality is that sometimes the waves do crash in. sometimes it feels like we are barely keeping our heads above the water. sometimes we feel lost at sea. sometimes we have to deal with very stormy weather.

and that is actually normal. even though it really sucks.

when we find ourselves lost in the darkness it can feel like we are letting ourselves down... not honouring this work we've been doing, not working on our lighthouse.

so what do you do?

i say you don't do a thing. you retreat. you float. you keep your head up and you ride out the waves and the storms.

honour what you are going through. feel whatever it is you need to feel. hide in bed if you need to... hunker down and take care of your heart, soul, body, and brain.

and then when the storm calms, you can figure out what to do next.

you can come back to your lighthouse.

you can start from the beginning again if you need to - ignite your light all over again, and go through each of the components we've been talking about.

maybe you need to start from scratch. rebuild. remodel. move the whole freaking thing to a new location!

or maybe you just need to open the door and come back inside. take one more little step up that spiral staircase, closer to your light once again.

the darkness is a gateway to the light. you can't hide from it. you can't get around it. you need to go through it and come out the other side.

building a lighthouse doesn't mean the darkness ceases to exist, it just means we have the tools - the light - to work through the darkness when it does creep up on us, and it will.

the shadows

sometimes knowing that you want to build your lighthouse and you are ready to shine your light is not quite enough.

it can sometimes feel like we are merely watching from the sidelines... in the shadow of the lighthouse itself. so close, but just not there yet, just not quite able to get inside.

and that feeling is agony... to have the vision of what we want for ourselves, and feel like we might be letting it slip away. standing in the shadows can feel a lot like you are on the outside looking in.

when i first read the quote that inspired my own lighthouse journey and began to explore what it would be like to shine, i certainly made some changes in my business and life that made a big difference. i got my mojo back... i found my spark again! i felt like i was much closer to living my purpose once i embraced teaching again and i felt more comfortable, more authentic with my work and my message.

but, as i have mentioned, i still felt like there was something missing. my business was a success, and i was proud of the progress i had made in my journey, but it still didn't feel like the lighthouse that i was longing to build.

i remember feeling really frustrated at the time. i had an amazing platform and reputation, i was earning money doing work that was really helpful to people, i was grateful to be working from home so i could be there for my kids, but i still felt like there must be more to the story.

i couldn't verbalize those feelings very well, but when i would have conversations with my friends or my peers i would have this feeling inside me like i just wanted to shout: "but is this what you really want? we're just going through the motions! we are just ticking boxes! we are just doing the same old things day in and day out and nothing changes! shouldn't there be something more than this?"

it didn't make sense to me at the time. i felt like i should be happy, grateful, content... fine. but instead i was dissatisfied.

i went back to my light... i went back to explore my purpose further and to think once again about what it was i really wanted to do in the world.

i thought about that feeling i was experiencing, of being on the outside looking in... of feeling like i was merely standing in the shadow of my lighthouse.

this feeling was strongest when i would see world class speakers who were lighting up the world with their messages... when i would see incredible thought leaders who were known for their innovative, world-changing ideas... when i would meet talented healers and teachers who had clear methods that were making a big difference to people's lives.

i realized that all of these people and messages and ideas were pointing me to what i wanted and where i wanted to go next.

and i also realized that even as i was standing in the shadows, that i was already doing some of what i truly wanted without even being aware of it. as i've mentioned previously, the times i felt the most lit up in my business were when i was talking to women about owning their light in the world and clearing away their resistance to their light.

so even if you are not feeling very lit up right now you can actually learn a lot from what you are doing in the shadows of your lighthouse. the shadows are a reminder that it might be time to go back to you... go back to your light... explore a little more what lights you up... and maybe even dream a little bigger.

the tides

throughout this whole journey i have definitely experienced both highs and lows. i went from having a teaching career that i loved to wanting to run away from going back to work. from having a completely booked out photography business to having no mojo at all to do the photo sessions. from having a thriving business teaching branding and marketing strategy to feeling like the heart and soul was missing from my work.

as i am sure every single one of us has experienced at different times, i have had wonderful successes and massive failures... i have felt absolutely ignited and absolutely stuck in the darkness.

the harbour of my lighthouse reminds me that this ebb and flow is just a normal part of the journey. in fact i think the ebbs and flows are needed... how do we know what our light needs to be if we've never experienced the darkness? how will we find the treasures left behind in the sand if there are only ever high tides?

what i am searching for now is a little bit of balance... to get away from the belief that this work has to be an either/or situation and instead enjoy both sides of the duality: i can enjoy both strategy and soul in my business and life, i can have both financial success and personal fulfilment, i can be both in my head and in my heart, i can feel both completely grounded and absolutely in the flow.

experiencing both the ups and downs has prompted me to seek and settle into my own happy middle. i am ready to find joy, love, peace, growth, inspiration, and authenticity in both the light AND the darkness... i believe it's possible.

i know that many people reading this book will be in a place that absolutely feels too dark to climb out of right now. some of you will have a foundation that feels like it is about to crumble at any moment, and wonder how you can possibly build a lighthouse with that. some of you will feel like the waves have been crashing in on you for so long now that you can hardly catch your breath.

for you, it might feel like simply surviving has been your purpose. and how then does one even begin to find the light again?

if this feels like your story right now, then the first thing i want you to do is close your eyes and take a deep breath and just know this: you are surrounded by an ocean of love.

and the next is to please remember that everything you've experienced so far has brought you to this moment, right now, which is exactly where you are meant to be.

your life and your experiences have made you who you are... being you and honouring who you are is exactly how you ignite your light. you can take one step forwards now, you can grow and ignite from this space... the wounded place in you is exactly where your light can enter.

and the very best thing is that when you own your light in the world, you give other people permission to do the same.

this means that when you choose today to take one little step out of the depths of darkness and into the shallows towards your light, you are not only changing the patterns and cycles of your own life, it creates a shift for everyone around you: your kids, your grandkids, your parents, your partner, your friends... for all of your loved ones.

just as the tides of the ocean flow in and out... there is a time and a phase for everything. it just might be time now to let go of that awful weight that has kept you tossing and turning out at sea for so long now, and find the treasure in the life that is waiting for you now.

your lighthouse is the guiding light that is calling you home.

surrender

one day i posted this message on social media: "today the lighthouse is reminding me that i don't have to be shiny and bright all the time... today i can let the other lighthouses in my life shine bright for me."

it had been a tough couple of weeks for me, personally. i had just travelled across the world to canada to have one last visit with my beloved grandma, who passed away just four days after my return to australia.

even though i planned for a long five-week trip overseas, even though i had a beautiful goodbye and some closure, even though i knew it was coming... nothing really prepares you for the impact it will have to lose a light in your life.

everything in my business and in my life kind of came to a standstill for a while... i needed to give myself time and space to just BE.

in that same time period i talked with a friend who had been struggling under the weight of depression, who hadn't been able to do a single thing to ignite her spark or explore her passion, because she literally just couldn't do a single thing.

i talked with a friend who was feeling a bit lost, with no direction, so she was just taking a break and spending time exploring her creativity. she was worried what impact the break would have on the business she just started, if she would lose momentum, lose trust.

i talked with a friend who was feeling ignited with a new passion, but had to put all of her ideas and plans on the back burner while she just coped with life and family and kids and home and all of the other responsibilities that seemed to take priority.

i talked with a friend who had lost his mojo for writing after some setbacks and some disappointing results. he'd retreated into life as a stay at home dad and was wondering how to get back on the horse, get back to creating and dreaming big.

the reason i wanted to share these stories is because i think we ALL have a story we could share about a time when we just couldn't work on our stuff. when we had to give ourselves a break. you might be experiencing it right this minute.

you are not alone. and it's ok.

you cannot take care of anything or anyone else until you take care of you. you do not have to shine all the time. you can surrender to whatever it is that is going on with you right now. you can just stand there. you can just BE.

sometimes we feel like we just have to push all the time - focus on the outcome, focus on the destination, focus on the result.

i have heard it called *efforting* - and i love that word. we all engage in so much efforting. and it's just not always possible to keep that up! it's not actually sustainable to keep that up.

sometimes we need to surrender.

we need to stop pushing and efforting and working so damn hard to figure it all out and keep it all going. we need to let go of our attachment to things working out a certain way or in a certain time period. we need to let go of all of the stuff we are desperately hanging on to... we need to set ourselves free.

we need to allow ourselves to just *be*.

i find that when these moments come it helps to surround yourself with other lighthouses.

surround yourself with souls that get you and get what you are going through, without judgement. they will help you to keep going, or at least keep standing, even during those times when it all is too hard. surround yourself with people who will keep shining bright even when you can't.

when all of the other lights are shining it is ok for you to switch yours off for a little while.

but never ever doubt that your light is indeed needed.

don't let yourself sink into a space where you wonder why you even bother, or wonder if what you do even matters. that space where you compare your lighthouse to others or begin to feel like it would just be easier to stay small and unseen.

to surrender does not mean to give up. to surrender simply means to let go of all of the resistance and control, the efforting and the pushing... to simply just float for a while and let the current take you back home to your light.

belonging

one of the comments that has come up a few times as i have been talking about the lighthouse as a symbol for our life, is that it reminds people of isolation.

i certainly know the feeling well... it feels a bit like you are on a little island all by yourself as you do this work and build a new life for yourself.

it can feel like no one really understands why you want to change your life in the first place; it can feel like people just don't 'get' the stuff you are working on or that you care about now; and it can even feel like some people don't want you to change at all.

what we will often do is keep this work to ourselves, and do this work by ourselves, so i can definitely see how the lighthouse reminds people of isolation.

and i am not going to tell you: "well just go put yourself out there. make some new friends. there are local groups, there are online groups, you don't have to be alone!" blah blah blah.

we've all heard it already, and let's be honest, those sorts of platitudes are just annoying.

i remember when i first moved to australia, hearing the same sort of thing when i would say i was lonely: "go to a playgroup. make some friends."

sure, you can put yourself out there and make some friends. yes, you can get invited out to the coffee shop or over for a play date. but what i wanted was a *real* friend - the kind you can phone in the middle of the day and say, "it's been a shit day and life is fucking hard and what i need most is to go out somewhere and have a beer. you in?"

it took me a while to find those friends, but i did.

but then, even when i had made some new, wonderful friends, i still felt isolated sometimes. once i had started working on my lighthouse i felt like i didn't really have people who i could have the deep soul conversations with: the conversations about purpose and love and intuition and feeling ignited (instead of, "hey, let's bitch about everything that is irritating us and lament about how much life sucks.")

it took me a while to find those friends, but i did. thank god.

so i am not going to tell you just to go out and find those people. i know how damned hard it is.

what i will say is that just because you might be feeling isolated, it doesn't mean you are alone.

we all are connected - each one of us who is working on our lighthouse, building something bigger and more empowering and more ignited for ourselves, travelling on this crazy journey - we are connected by our desire to own our light in the world.

one of the reasons i started the lighthouse revolution was to build a wonderful community of people who could support each other and cheer each other on... where we could say, "i'm working on my lighthouse," and other people would get it!

there is one thing that has made a big difference to me in connecting with people who care about the same stuff i do - people who i could go out for a beer with AND have those wonderful, igniting-your-soul types of conversations.

vulnerability.

showing who i really am. being real about what i am really going through. sharing how i really feel.

but i won't lie... it is scary.

what if i turn people off?

what if i look like a loser or some kind of woo-woo crack pot?

what if i start to cry and my friends think i have completely lost the plot?

what i noticed is that before i started to open up to people in a really authentic, vulnerable way, all interactions felt either like they were on the surface or they were merely strategic... nice enough, but there was still something missing.

when i allowed myself to be vulnerable and admit things to my friends that really mattered to me, to talk about the stuff that was either lighting me up or feeling like the darkness, everything changed.

the people who i have been most vulnerable with are now my strongest supporters, my loveliest friends, and the people i can, without a doubt, call up to go for a beer and a soul chat.

have a look around you. there is someone who is longing for a deeper connection just as you are. perhaps it's time to give them, and yourself, a chance.

just remember, though we may be working on our lighthouse all on our own, we are connected to each of those women who are doing the same. let their light be a signal to you... you are not alone.

surround yourself with other lighthouse keepers... ones who support you and also inspire you. ones that are a reflection of the light you have to shine.

stand tall in your harbour... remember that you are part of a community and allow yourself to feel a sense of belonging.

feel protected by the lighthouses you see being built around you, feel supported by the lighthouse keepers in your life, feel secure in your place here.

i think it is such a beautiful thing to close my eyes and picture a long shoreline scattered with the lights of many lighthouses, standing tall and shining bright.

the ocean is vast and wide, there is room for all of us.

and in fact, your light is needed too... otherwise there would be a big gap on that shoreline without any light at all (a gap in your home, a gap in your community, a gap in your niche or workplace or friendship group.)

together - we have more power.

together - we can light up the whole world.

your compass

we each are born with our very own inner compass... our intuition. we all have it, though not all of us are adept at reading our own compass, or recognizing that it is even there.

looking back on my life there were definitely times when my intuition was absolutely switched ON and i was tuned into the feeling.

i can remember just knowing that a friend was in trouble. i can remember feeling like something bad had happened and i needed to call home. i can remember the zing i got when i walked in the room and met my future husband.

so i've definitely always had that intuition - we all have it! - but like many people, i had forgotten what my intuition felt like most of the time. i had forgotten how to tune in and listen to that inner knowing.

as i began to find my spark again, and began to build the lighthouse that would help me to shine my light, i also began to tune back into my intuition.

those crazy dreams i mentioned at the start of the book were a pretty big kick in the pants for me. when i discovered the meaning of those dreams - when i realized that my instinct was correct and they were in fact different to the regular dreams we all have - and when i understood that they were from my inner soul trying to get a message to me for over 10 years! - well that was a big wake-up call for me... it was time to learn how to tune into my intuition and listen to my own inner knowing.

plus it was confirmation that the niggling feeling i had about those dreams all along was real... *that* was the feeling of my intuition.

one way that my intuition works is via messages from music, lyrics, quotes, articles, and people.

i don't know *how* i know, i just know when something is not random, when instead it is a message meant for me. that niggling feeling that i am learning to trust is there at certain times and i just *know*.

sometimes when i am feeling stuck with something i will simply ask out loud: "ok, i really need some help here. if you've got any insight for me please do share! i am open and ready to receive."

and then i just keep my eyes and ears open and make note of what comes my way. i feel like i am on a bit of a treasure hunt... what clues will i happen upon today?

if i am on my phone, scrolling around online, i will take a screen shot of anything that gives me that niggling feeling. if i'm not on my phone, i will note things in my journal. once i do, i often begin to notice trends: i look for any coincidences, moments of synchronicity, and any patterns or repetition that seem to occur.

and here is the most important part - i always say thank you! out loud i will say: "oh yes! message received! thank you! please keep sending more stuff like that or even better!"

i feel like when you acknowledge that intuition it strengthens the whole experience - the feeling or knowing (or seeing or hearing or however it is you receive information) gets cemented in as real as any other sense.

and it creates an anchor: something you can hold on to, something you can come back to. each time your intuition kicks in you will become more and more aware of it, more trusting of it, more in tune with it.

i note in my journal when i do have that niggling feeling or receive any messages as well as noting how i acted on them and what the outcome was. something as simple as: *had a random urge to call a friend and found out that she was really lonely and needed someone to talk to. BINGO! once again, intuition is right! thank you!* simple acknowledgement builds trust in yourself, in that feeling, that inner knowing.

a compass is one of the most important tools available to us as we go on this journey.

it will help us to be true to ourselves. it will help us to make decisions and navigate our path. it will help us to overcome obstacles and take inspired action. it will help us to find our way to our light.

your inner light, your inner knowing, becomes your compass.

when you trust in it, and when you know how it feels and works for you, you can rely on it to show you the way back home... back to you.

a few months ago i was planning a trip home to canada and really struggling with how i was going to fit in all of the travel and visiting i needed to do, especially as i was travelling with three kids on my own. we were planning to attend a big family reunion, and also wanted to be present for the interment of my grandmother's ashes, as we weren't able to attend her funeral months before.

trying to organize everything with multiple family members was beginning to stress me out. one morning i was off to have a coffee with a friend and hopped in the car with all of this stress on my mind. as i was driving, a song about the rain came on the radio - some random song that i had no real connection to - and i had the thought pop in my head that my grandma loved the rain.

i kept driving. the next song to come on the radio was also about the rain. i just laughed out loud... i knew then that grandma was there with me. the next three songs to come on the radio sent a very clear message: *listen to your heart* - do what you need to do, and don't worry about anything or anyone else. *because i am right here with you* - all the time, you don't need to come see me in a cemetery! *don't stop believing* - remember, you can close your eyes any time and i am here with you.

and after that last song was over i knew the message was over too - i had a sense that it was done, that the next song was just a song.

it was a remarkable moment.

now someone might say: "that is a load of bullshit; you could come up with any message you want from a string of songs on the radio." and that's fine - whatever suits you. we each get to believe exactly what we choose to believe.

but for me - now that i've opened up my intuition again - i see these moments as little bits of magic in my life. i find it FUN and joyful and awesome to experience the world in this way.

each little moment or experience of magic that happens in any given day is just one more little spark that helps me to light up my lighthouse.

grounding

as i've mentioned, i spend a lot of time in my head. my brain is constantly on the go - figuring things out, putting puzzle pieces together, learning and sorting and organizing. the constant streaming, never-ending to do list.

it can leave me feeling like my head is in the clouds. that i am not fully present... instead distracted and feeling frazzled.

the trouble with this is that i spend so much time thinking and figuring - always seven steps ahead in my mind - not enough time just BEing. and i've learnt that it's hard to shine your light when you aren't even really present in the moment. it creates a feeling of disconnect, dissatisfaction... distance between you and your light.

you are exactly where you are supposed to be. so be there!

when i catch myself in this state, i remember that i need to be where my feet are.

i need to come back to my harbour, back to myself.

i need to get grounded.

i am not naturally very good at grounding... but i am definitely learning strategies to get better at it, because i find that it really does make a difference.

a great little mindfulness exercise that i find very helpful is to say out loud: *i am here, i am aware.* and then simply name out loud everything i can see around me... everything present in the moment.

even better, try to enjoy the moment: *isn't this moment wonderful?* isn't this beautiful or peaceful or absolutely perfect or so very lucky. basically, i say something out loud that brings me back to the here and now, and out of the chaos of my mind.

this can also work if i find myself dwelling on the past or living in the future, instead of simply being in the present moment. or if i find myself dwelling on work while i am at home with my family or stressing over home responsibilities when i'm out with friends... or whatever.

anything that is taking you out of the moment and into your head can add to that feeling of chaotic frenzy... of madly treading water just to keep your head up.

another situation where grounding is really important to me, is when i find that i am taking on too much energy from the outside world.

i am a sensitive person... i feel things deeply. so when there is a lot of negativity in my social feed or tragedy in the news, i take that on myself, i feel like it is actually happening to me. i am one of those people that never ever clicks on a link if it says: "oh, this is so sweet, you must watch!" 'so sweet' to the average person equals 'the ugly cry' for me. so i don't watch the news, i don't watch or read stuff that i know is just going make me cry. i try to surround myself with stuff that lights me up, lifts me higher.

and when i am closely connected with others i can find myself really feeling the stuff they are going through. the more i have become aware of this, the more i have discovered just how often it happens.

one time, in a meeting at school, i could feel the frustration of another parent like a tidal wave coming right at me. another time, after holding a one-day workshop for women in business, i couldn't sleep for the waves of inspiration and idea generation and excited fear that i was experiencing… not my own but from the other attendees! at a conference once i felt so much anxiety and nervousness from one of the speakers on stage, and so much love and devotion being pushed out from her avid fans, that i felt quite overwhelmed.

this sort of energy can leave me feeling quite out of sorts… lost at sea. it's hard enough to deal with our own stuff, let alone other people's stuff!

when this happens i know that i have to come back to me.

i take deep, centering breaths and picture my light as a little ball of energy inside of me, near my heart, glowing brightly as though i am lit from within. then i picture the light expanding outwards. i picture sending it out, like little beams, to the people who have the anxiety, nervousness, or frustration, and when the light is flowing outwards, none of that stuff can be sneaking back inwards to me (just like water can only flow one way through a hose.) i also picture the light flowing through me, down through my feet, to the ground… anchoring me in my own body, and into the present moment.

when you find yourself feeling frazzled or out of sorts, when you want to quiet your mind or check in with your energy...

breathe. be where your feet are. come back to you. come back to your light.

space

how many things do you have on your to do list right now? how many balls are you juggling in the air right now? how many items are going through your mind right now?

most of us would probably answer 'too many' but we would also say that it's just how life is right now. many of us are juggling multiple jobs: as parents or caregivers, as employees or employers, as business builders or community builders, as partners or friends or family members.

life is busy, right?

the trouble is, when we have no space at all, any-where in our lives, when we are booked solid from morning to night working on the multiple to do lists running through our minds, that is when we can find ourselves the most stuck.

warning: lack of space may cause stuckness

it can show up in your life in a variety of ways... lost mojo, writer's block/creativity blocks, lack of clarity/focus, procrastination, low productivity, self-doubt, and more.

the funny thing is that when faced with one or more of those situations we tend to 'soldier on,' when what we might need the most is just to stop altogether. at least for a little while.

to create space.

there are no rules for what 'space' needs to look like.

go for a walk. have a hot bath. take an extra-long shower. jump on the trampoline. listen to music. run. do yoga. meditate. play. colour. doodle. journal. sit. nap. vacation. have wine with a girlfriend. read something just for fun. lay on the grass. float in the waves. visit a church or a sacred space.

basically, anything that doesn't feel like another item on your to do list or another ball you are juggling? that's space.

slow down... give yourself the gift of a moment of space.

i'm going to be totally honest here... this is one of the topics in this book that i often struggle with myself. my 'go to' state is constant busy-ness, and the thought that most often runs through my head is something along the lines of: "to much to do, not enough time! i just don't have time for that!"

then, when i get completely overwhelmed and stuck, my go to state becomes absolute inertia - i just want to hide in my bed with a trashy novel, never to surface again.

and let me tell you, i get really twitchy when some-one tells me: "you know, you need to take some time for yourself." (because i am a rebel and i don't like being told what to do, and also... as if that thought hadn't already occurred to me... didn't you hear me, i have no time!)

but now that i have started building my lighthouse - now that i understand better the work i need to do in order to shine my light in the world - i can see how important space is. i just need to do it my way.

i've always loved walking at the beach; i don't go to church, but i would say that the ocean is absolutely my version of a church... it's my sacred space. it's definitely where i feel like i can both get grounded and find space.

i also love reading, yoga, meditation, writing in my journal... i even love just sitting in my car for a few quiet moments looking out at the sea or having extra-long showers with the door locked so i can't hear a thing happening in the house.

these are activities that feel really spacious to me, and i know my life is better when i have these. but i need to be sure i allow time for them. i need to fiercely protect that time so that it doesn't get knocked to the bottom of another to do list.

recently, i have been playing around with deepening my spiritual practice... spending some time out of my head and in my heart and soul instead. the advice i was given by someone who knows me well was: do not make this another thing you have to put on your to do list, figure out, or puzzle-piece together. this is meant to be a way to create space and flow and get unstuck... so making it a chore is counter intuitive!

so i have just been treating this as time to play, to explore, to be curious and experiment and see what feels like *me* and feels like fun and seems to work. i've been playing with meditation & prayer, reiki & chakras, crystals & essential oils, oracle cards & angel cards, and more... discovering so many fun ways to connect with my soul and connect with the universe.

but, because i've been completely treating this as 'play time,' as soon as life got busy it was the first thing to get pushed out of my day; i did not protect this time or space. i went from having soulful play time every morning for a few weeks to suddenly not doing anything but work and taking care of everyone else and everything else but me.

remember the story about my weird dream? the alarm clock going off to remind me to listen to my heart and my soul? well that dream came back with a vengeance - multiple times in one night i woke up in a panic, having lost or forgotten something important which was hidden away in the bottom of my shelf.

the whole next day i felt unsettled, frazzled, and very unproductive... not to mention short tempered and short on patience. i was in the middle of complaining to my friend about how hard everything was - the usual bitching about too much to do and not enough time - then it hit me, as all 'ah ha' moments do.

the dream. i had forgotten myself, once again. i had been having fun creating this spiritual practice and as soon as i got busy and stressed i just pushed that down to the bottom of the priority list... the bottom shelf. the thing i needed to make time for the most was forgotten due to feeling like i had no time.

so i got back into the practice and now make time for myself every day, even if it isn't as long as i would like it to be. it's not always easy - our lives do get so busy! but i know that if i don't make time to be a human BEing for a while (instead of always a human DOing) it's very detrimental to my life... i am not the best version of myself without some space for me.

space creates flow again. 'flow' is the opposite of 'stuck.'

we need to give our ideas space to grow; we need space for creation and creativity; space allows the next steps of our path to present themselves; space provides opportunity for processing, regrouping, reflection, self-care, intuition, nourishment, rest... all things our minds, souls, and bodies need!

picture the lighthouse in your mind's eye.

is it placed in the middle of a block of high-rise buildings?

is it surrounded by crazy, thronging crowds?

nope.

it's just pure space.

what can you do right now to create a little space for yourself?

the horizon

we live in a little suburb in the south of adelaide, australia... we rent a modest house and make a modest living. but there is one thing that makes me feel rich and abundant...

we are on a bit of a hill, and the back of our house faces west; just over the houses and the highway we can even see a little peek of the sea. and most nights we get to witness the most beautiful sunsets.

my hubby and kids often laugh at me as i run out-side each evening to say: look at the sunset - it is so amazing! "we know, mom, we know!"

but the sunset has come to mean something more to me than simple stunning beauty (which is very grounding in and of itself.)

for me, the sunset reminds me to be grateful.

each time i witness the sun set in that gorgeous sky, especially over the sea, i just feel so damned lucky! i always try to do a little mental tally of all of the stuff in my life that i am so grateful for.

i live in a place where i feel safe and loved. i have amazing family and friends in my life... near and far. i have my health and the health of those i love. i have the freedom to be at home with my babies, witnessing their growth into freaking awesome human beings. i get to be my own boss. i feel ignited by the work i do and the life i live.

let's face it, this isn't always an easy gig. i will be completely honest: there are lots of days those same babies drive me close to insanity. lots of days i feel homesick for my family and friends in canada. lots of days where my relationships feel like hard work or my business feels like hard work or i don't feel very successful or very effective.

lots of days where i don't feel very lit up at all.

but then the sunset will just give me that moment of pause - that moment to remember the many things i have to be grateful for, to appreciate the abundance in my life.

and that moment to remember that tomorrow is a brand new day.

i can start fresh. i can start again.

i can accept a new invitation to shine.

tomorrow doesn't have to be like today if i don't want it to be - i can start fresh and do things differently.

or if today has been an awesome day, tomorrow can be just as awesome or even better. there are no limits to the number of awesome days we get to have. just because things are great doesn't mean they will crash and burn at the next turn.

even in a storm we can choose to see the beauty in our harbour. we can be reminded as the sun sets and rises over the sea that how we see the world is up to us.

we can also look out over the horizon and choose to believe that the universe has our back.

again - being absolutely transparent here - there are lots of times i get stuck in my head. in the ego 'poor me... me me me' place.

the world hates me. this is such a shit day. why is this happening to me? it feels like i am destined to fail. no matter what i try, nothing works. wahhhhh. life sucks!

it's not a very shiny place to be.

but the harbour reminds me to come back home again, come back to my light.

i am exactly where i am meant to be.

the universe has my back - even if i might not understand it now, everything happens for a reason, and it is all for my highest good.

all is well.

a funny thing is, i have always had the belief that everything happens for a reason. when it comes to things like your car breaking down, a job or house application not turning out the way you wanted it to, vacation plans going awry... i trust that it all happens for a reason.

but when it comes to me personally... not so much.

it doesn't make sense. i can say, "oh well, it didn't turn out," when it comes to so many random things in life. but if one of my own efforts or projects is an utter flop - oh, it's the end of the world! i suck! the universe hates me!

i've had to train myself to flip my thinking. to have that same faith that the universe has my back on this journey i am on - just as it would if i was on vacation!

i have been trying to become less attached to the outcome, in all things in life, but especially when it comes to my own goals and plans.

to trust that everything works out for my greater good.

that i am indeed exactly where i am meant to be.

and all is well.

your anchor

we started this book with igniting our light. and doesn't that just feel so damn good? to follow what lights you up, to feel like you've found your purpose, to have a beautiful big vision for yourself of what you want from your life and why.

i love being in that high vibe energy - it makes me feel like i've totally got my mojo, like the whole world is open to me.

but as we've already said, you don't live in the light all of the time, you also have to live in the darkness... sometimes you feel like you've lost your way, sometimes you feel like the waves are crashing in.

in these cases i find that it helps to have an anchor. something to hang on to, something that will allow me to return to my light as quickly as i can, something to remind me of that high vibe feeling that fuels this journey.

an anchor can be anything: a symbol; a physical object; a colour; a scent; a word, phrase, or mantra; a song; a photograph; an animal; or even a person!

i have all sorts of anchors. i often choose crystals that have particular meanings, i like to wear them and hold them to help me remember my intention. i also have a number of pieces of jewellery that hold different meanings to me, they act as anchors for different things in my life. i also love using essential oils and particular scents have become anchors for different intentions.

music, as i have mentioned, is very meaningful to me and i have created a whole playlist of music for the lighthouse revolution on spotify - sometimes i will put it on random and just see what message i need to be reminded of that day; sometimes i will choose a song on purpose, play it very loud and sing at the top of my lungs. that is a sure fire way to get back to my intention and raise my vibration!

(you can listen to the lighthouse revolution playlist on spotify - choose a song from the list to be your anchor! grab it and other lighthouse revolution freebies at karengunton.com)

you can choose an anchor right now to represent the life you want to build for yourself. you can pick one for each of your dreams and goals. you can pick one to set an intention for your day, your week, your month, or your year. you can choose one for each area of your life. you can use this idea however you want - the main thing is just to have some sort of talisman or physical touchstone that will help you remember who you want to be in the world... the light you wish to shine.

you can also turn any moment, memory, or experience into an anchor. i shared earlier my story about getting to visit the set of my favourite TV show and then having the song from the show come on the radio just as got in my car to go home that night. that moment is an anchor - if i ever need to be reminded of what it feels like when my dreams come true and i know that the universe has my back - i take a minute to remember that exact moment and how i felt, and yep, i even sing the song at the top of my lungs.

i will do the same when i know that my intuition is on fire, or i am receiving messages from the universe, or my body is trying to tell me something in some way - i try to anchor those moments in my memory so that i can more easily recognize them and honour them when it happens again.

to anchor moments like that in your mind, write them down or take a photo or make note of the song that is playing or a scent that is in the air or something you are wearing. those physical talismans can really help you get right back to that amazing feeling once again (as i am sure you've noticed if you already have scents or songs or symbols that remind you of people or times in your life.)

anchors are a wonderful way to remember the light you are here to shine, the world you are longing to build for yourself. the journey is not always easy - so give yourself something solid and powerful to hang on to as you ride the waves.

the harbour reminds us that though we may not always be living in the light, we can come back to it at any time. the darkness, the shadows, the tides, and the waves are all part of this journey, but our lighthouse is a guiding light pointing our way back home and our anchors will allow us to hang on and come back to our light at any time.

look up at the sky above.

seek your source.

this is bigger than you.

trust in the universe.

have faith.

be a clear channel.

raise your vibration.

connect to your light.

part 7

light up

the lighthouse has unfolded for me in the order that i wrote about it here.

i started out asking the questions: "what does it mean to shine? how do we ignite our spark? how do we find ourselves again and learn what lights us up?"

once i began to feel more authentic, more on purpose, more ignited... it was much easier to beam my light out there, to find my voice and to be visible.

(it makes sense - you can't beam your light if you haven't got the light switched on in the first place!)

very quickly it became apparent that there were some things in my work and my life that weren't really aligned any more, that no longer served me. so the next step was really about building the tower.

and truthfully, i was working on these first three components for a long time. at first, my focus was all on my business: igniting my light, being a beacon, and building my tower were really the way that i built a successful online business teaching women about business.

but over time i realized that there had to be something more - there had to be something else i was missing - and that is when i came back to the lighthouse to see what other lessons there were to learn.

by this time i realized that building our mindset is as much our job as anything else on our 'to do' list, and so building a foundation became an essential part of my journey.

and that led me to thinking about all of the stuff that comes up and gets us, and how often we choose to just stay stuck or go back to being safe and small and comfy.

visualizing the spiral staircase as a symbol of our journey was one of the most empowering things i could learn from the lighthouse... to understand that we are on this journey to deal with stuff and to grow, and that it is our choice to take one more little step towards the light.

the harbour has been the most recent component of the lighthouse to unfold... it was only when i was in a really dark place myself that i truly understood the shadow side to the lighthouse, and how our own light acts as a guide to point us back home again.

because this is the order the components appeared to me, this is the order that i always share them with everyone else... i always start with igniting your light and work through the components from there.

and so i always urge people who are feeling stuck to do just that - get back to you, get back to your light, and then go through each component of the lighthouse and see what comes up for you.

build YOUR lighthouse

of course, you can go through the components of your lighthouse in any order you want. if you are working on finding and igniting your light and right away can see how you need to build your mindset - go do that! strengthen your foundation! awesome plan.

and of course, the components are all intertwined. there are lots of overlapping themes and ideas, and you might find that each component brings up some different meanings and symbols for you.

that is awesome too.

the beauty of the lighthouse as a symbol for the lives we are building, is that no two lighthouses are alike! each one is absolutely perfect for its location, it's purpose, it's harbour.

the lighthouse doesn't actually worry about what any of the other lighthouses are doing up and down the shoreline... it just stands there shining.

so you get to take this idea - this symbol - and do what works for you. make it your own. build YOUR lighthouse.

start today.

you can start by thinking of your whole life in general.

- work on igniting your light... finding you and BEING you and seeing your own light clearly

- then allow yourself to be a beacon... being visible and raising your voice, owning your truth and SHARING you.

- consider how you can build your tower... one that SERVES you, with alignment and integrity.

- then work on strengthening your foundation... BUILDING you, building your mindset

- remember the spiral staircase... accept that all of the stuff that comes up is part of the JOURNEY, be aware of what your stuff is, and keep taking those steps to work through it all.

- and when things get tough, when the waves get rough... COME BACK to you, come back to your safe harbour.

or, if you want, you can just pick one thing in your life that you want to concentrate on right now.

a goal you have, a project you are working on, something new you want to try, a thing that has been tapping you on the shoulder for a long time.

maybe it is about health & fitness, perhaps it is about your relationships, it could be a new hobby or interest, it might be about your work or business, it could be a project like writing a book... pick that *one thing* that has been niggling at you.

then go through each component of the lighthouse with that one thing in mind and see what comes up for you... see what you can learn from the lighthouse, see what you can start working on today.

(to help, you can use the printable, one-page lighthouse blueprint which is a bonus with this book. grab it and other lighthouse revolution freebies at karengunton.com)

i love that you can apply the lessons of the lighthouse to your life as a whole and you can also apply them to single aspects of your life... to anything you like really!

what happened for me is that i started working on making my business my lighthouse - and i still do use these six components in my business all the time. anytime i plan for the year, start a new pro-ject, or even just feel stuck in some way, i ask: "ok, what does the lighthouse have to teach me here?" and i go through each of the components.

but over time i began to see that that one thing - my business - is actually just one part of my light-house (not the whole thing!)

the lighthouse is ME - i am the lighthouse. my business is one part of my tower, one way that i ignite my light and be a beacon and build my foun-dation... one part of this journey that i am on.

but there are other parts of my life that need to be part of my lighthouse too. my relationships, my home, my health, my self-care, my interests and activities... they are all part of this journey.

once i began to apply the lessons of the lighthouse to one thing (my business), the other things in my life began to shift as well.

because all of this is indeed intertwined.

your life is a reflection of you.

when you build you, you build your life, and vice versa.

when you transform one part of your life, other things will transform (or need to transform) as well.

so in the end that is what the lighthouse has done for me.

i wanted to stand tall and shine bright. i wanted to find my soul's purpose and feel lit up from within. but as i mentioned earlier, my brain always asks, "but how?"

building a lighthouse is how.

it's got all of the lessons i will need on this journey...

and so i shall build my lighthouse.

and so i shall BE the lighthouse.

the sky above

there is one more aspect of this journey that i am only just beginning to understand, explore, and relate to the lighthouse; when i look up at the big, beautiful sky above, i am reminded of this one thing...

this is bigger than me.

the more i work on building my lighthouse, the more i explore what it means to own my light in the world, the more i realize that the light doesn't come *from* me... it comes *through* me.

i am simply a channel for light to shine through.

i am not a religious person, i did not grow up in a religious home and i don't go to church. but i did grow up believing that there is something more... something bigger than each of us, something beautiful and wonderful and all-encompassing that we are all a part of...

something that is the source of all light.

you can think of this source in any way that works for you... whatever aligns with your beliefs and the way choose you experience the world.

you can think of it as something inside of you: your soul or your intuition. you can think of it as something outside of you: your guides or your angels. you can think of it as something more universal: god, spirit, divine, or the universe. you can even just simply think of it as source. call it whatever you like, it's completely up to you.

it doesn't matter what you call it because in the end it is all the same thing... it is the source of our light. we are all connected to it, we are all equal no matter what our beliefs... no matter how we choose to shine. we get to connect in any way that makes us feel connected... we get to do spirituality in any way we choose.

you might already be in a place in your journey where seeking and connecting to your source is important to you. you might be like me, and not really explore this at all until you have been working on the other components of your lighthouse for awhile.

perhaps you too will begin to sense that a connection to your own light is actually a connection to something bigger than you.

i've had quite a few moments over the years when i've been working on something, sharing something, or teaching something and i've had the thought: "i don't even know where all of that came from! it's like it just came to me... came *through* me."

and now i think i am beginning to understand that in a much deeper way.

when we work from a place of purpose... authenticity, alignment, genuine love, and connection... the light does just come right through us.

and when we work to build ourselves up, and work to clear away all of the blocks and negativity and fear and darkness... we clear the path for the light.

we become a clear channel for light.

we become a part of something much bigger than us.

so, when you are feeling like maybe this is all just too hard, and perhaps it is better to just stay safe and small and comfy.

when you wonder if you should even bother, since there are other people already doing it better and faster and bigger than you.

when it feels like it's a lot of work to get there because it's triggering all of your fears and blocks and issues.

when you are stuck in overwhelm, struggle, pressure, and exhaustion... buried under a mountain of to dos and should-dos and rules and advice.

when that voice in your head is whispering: "who are you to do this?" "you're not enough!" "you better give up now."

when you find yourself caught up in those stories you are telling yourself, dwelling on the past, or worrying about the future.

remember this: this journey is not all about *you*.

as gabby bernstein says: *"this not your business, this is god's business. you are the servant of something much bigger than you, something fucking unstoppable".* [22]

you are simply a channel, a vehicle... a lighthouse... for this light to shine through.

you are exactly where you are meant to be and you will be given everything you need.

the phrase *'let go and let god'* comes to mind. get out of your head... let go of all that stuff that's going on in there.

get back to your light.

get back to that high vibration energy of joy, peace, love, growth, inspiration and authenticity... be the light you wish to receive.

have faith that you are on this journey to your light for a reason, trust that the universe has your back.

your job is simply to show up. rise up. and light up.

join the lighthouse revolution

i hope that reading this story of the lighthouse and what it can teach us about shining our light in the world has inspired you to build a lighthouse of your own.

one of my favourite comments ever from a reader was when she told me that she asked her husband: "can you please take the kids for an hour or two? i need some time to work on my lighthouse."

i *love* that.

please make time to work on your lighthouse. please don't just put this book aside... now that you have heard the call to rise up and shine your light it's time to take some sort of courageous action. do the scary thing, push away from the shore, close your eyes and leap... because this is where the magic happens.

you should also know that this work is never really done... you don't just build your lighthouse and then forget about it. i work on my lighthouse every day... i am constantly working on the lessons and strategies that i have shared here.

if you want something awesome to happen, you need to do something awesome! you need to put some light out into the world. you need to show up and be prepared to do the work.

i would love for you to visit karengunton.com and join the lighthouse revolution. i have some awesome freebies for you there as companions to this book: a beautiful lighthouse revolution manifesto based on the messages in this book, the lighthouse revolution spotify playlist, a guided lighthouse visualization recording, a printable one page blueprint to help you build your lighthouse, and more! we also have an amazing online community for you to connect with other lighthouse keepers.

i would also like to share with you my secret dream... the one that lives deep inside of me. my dream is for you, gorgeous reader, to one day be talking with a friend, and when you hear that she is longing for something more in her life you will exclaim: "i know exactly what you need! you need to build a lighthouse!" maybe you will loan her your book, maybe you will invite her to our online community, maybe you will tell her your own story of how you are igniting your light.

my BIG dream is that the message of the lighthouse spreads far and wide. that together we will create ripples of light outwards from each person who chooses to light up and inspires someone else to do the same.

and please, always remember that you *do* have a light to shine.

the incredible wayne dyer[23] shared a very important message in his movie the shift: "*do not die with your music still inside you.*"

i implore you to remember that message, and will add: please do not die with your light still hidden, lost, or forgotten inside you.

light up.

it's what you were born to do.

build your lighthouse.

ignite your light. be you... authentically you. learn you. explore your purpose. know your why. define your dream. seek clarity. see your light.

be a beacon. share you. beam your light outwards. be visible. speak your truth. tell your stories. connect with your boats. own your light.

build your tower. serve you. seek alignment & integrity. choose simplicity. give yourself permission. do it your way. build what you love. love your light.

strengthen your foundation. build you. believe in yourself. expand out of your comfort zone. take action. stand tall. back yourself. support your light.

use the spiral staircase. it's your journey. step towards your light. clear your resistance. spiral with your stuff. keep marching on. rise above. honour your light.

find your harbour. come home. use your inner compass. ride out the storms. embrace the darkness. be grounded. hold on to your anchor. come back to your light.

look up at the sky above. seek your source. this is bigger than you. trust in the universe. have faith. be a clear channel. raise your vibration. connect to your light.

light up. shine bright.

(visit karengunton.com for a free, beautiful, printable poster of this manifesto)

acknowledgements

i never would have written, published, or launched this book without the support of so many awesome people in my life... seriously, it would have just stayed as one of those 'maybe someday' secret dreams, tapping me on the shoulder, ignored because of the impossibility of it all.

to my family: my husband james gunton; my children ella, taylor, and finn; my mom and dad, ken and leanne haltiner... thank you beautiful family for supporting me, believing in me, and allowing me to bring this book to life as i hid away in my office night after night. my greatest wish is that my children will grow up knowing what it means to live a life that lights them up and will have the courage to go after their own big dreams, having seen by example their mom doing just that.

to my friends: my very best besties - jenn craig, kelli dudley, and bruce james - as well as my uvic girls, my sheidow park girls, and my family girls... the conversations i have had with each of you are what showed me that the lighthouse could really make a difference to *all*... it could be bigger and beyond what i ever imagined to be possible. your love, support, and encouragement have meant more to me than i can possibly put into words, and your willingness to share your stories and explore your light with me has inspired and humbled me beyond measure. from the bottom of my heart, thank you.

to my support team: my product launch coach melanie sorenson, my editor assisi chant, my business coach tash corbin, my best biz buddy louisa gormley, my soulful friend clare fitzgerald, and my book writing buddy helen butler... thank you so much. your helpful advice, unparalleled skill, and unwavering support are what got this book out to the world. thank you also to the awesome book launch team who have helped with every decision and offered amazing encouragement along the way. i appreciate you joining me on this ride!

i have been so lucky to have met so many amazing women - both online and in person - who have made my life better and brighter. i would love to name every single one of you, but i fear it would be a very long list and i would still surely miss someone whom i adore. if you are an old friend or new... online or off... a fellow women in business, a mentor or a mastermind buddy, a client or customer, a member of the lighthouse revolution community group, or we have connected in some wonderful way... please know that i am so freaking grateful to know you, to be touched by your light. thank you for being part of this journey.

lastly, thank *you* gorgeous reader for joining me on this little tour of the lighthouse. i do hope it inspires you to build your own lighthouse and to be the highest, brightest version of yourself... thank you for joining the lighthouse revolution.

be sure to visit karengunton.com for some fun freebies to go along with the book!

keep shining,

karen xo

about the author

karen gunton is an unstucktor, an alchemist, and a badass rule-breaker who never uses capitals. she is on a mission to inspire women to seek their purpose, claim their dream, and own their light in the world. she started the lighthouse revolution as a call to action for women to create a shift in their life and start living a life that lights them up.

she lives in adelaide, australia with her husband and three children... though, every australian winter she chases the sun back to canada for some more summer fun. you can find her in her happy place: on the beach with a book in one hand, a cold beer in the other, and her bare toes in the sand.

find karen on facebook, instagram, and twitter @karengunton or at her website karengunton.com where you will find free resources and a free community for the lighthouse revolution. karen also offers a variety of online workshops, group programs, and personal sessions to help women build a lighthouse in their business or their life. karen is available as a keynote speaker, and/or workshop presenter for live events.

references

[1] Lamott, Anne. "The Last Class." Bird by Bird: Some Instructions on Writing and Life. New York: Anchor, 1995. 235. Print.

[2] Gilbert, Elizabeth. Big Magic: Creative Living beyond Fear. N.p.: Riverhead Books, 2015. Print.

[3] Coelho, Paulo. The Alchemist. San Francisco: HarperSanFrancisco, 1993. Print.

[4] Joseph, Jenny. Warning: When I Am an Old Woman I Shall Wear Purple. London: Souvenir, 1997. Print.

[5] Sinek, Simon. Start with Why: How Great Leaders Inspire Everyone to Take Action. New York: Portfolio, 2009. Print.

[6] Simon Sinek: How Great Leaders Inspire Action. TED.com, Sept. 2009. Web.

[7] Gray, Emma. "In Praise Of Women Who Give All The F**ks." HuffingtonPost.com, 8 May 2015. Web.

[8] Bernstein, Gabrielle. "How to Start a Movement." gabbybTV.com. May 2015. Web.

[9] Brown, Brene?. Daring Greatly: How the Courage to Be Vulnerable Transforms the Way We Live, Love, Parent, and Lead. New York, NY: Gotham, 2012. Print.

[10] Hendricks, Gay. The Big Leap: Conquer Your Hidden Fear and Take Life to the next Level. New York, NY: HarperCollins, 2009. Print.

[11] Duffield-Thomas, Denise. "The simple mantra to dramatically shift your self-worth." LuckyBitch.com. Nov. 2013. Web.

[12] *Tony Robbins: Why Some People Take Massive Action and Others Don't.* youtube.com, 13 Oct. 2015. Web.

[13] Winfrey, Oprah. *What I Know for Sure.* N.p.: Flatiron, 2014. Print.

[14] *Carol Dweck: The power of believing that you can improve.* TED.com, Nov. 2014. Web.

[15] Dooley, Mike. *Tut.com.* Web. 2016.

[16] Godin, Seth. "Tattoo Thinking." *sethgodin.typepad.com.* 22 Aug. 2012. Web.

[17] Wesely, Tommy. "Exclusive Q&A with Glee's Darren Criss | Teen Vogue." Teen Vogue. Conde Nast Digital, 23 Nov. 2010. Web. 14 Mar. 2016.

[18] Messenger, Lisa. *Daring and Disruptive: Unleashing the Entrepreneur.* Australia Square: Messenger Group, The., 2014. Print.

[19] Williamson, Marianne. *A Return to Love: Reflections on the Principles of a Course in Miracles.* New York: Harper-Collins, 1996. Print.

[20] *Joe Vitale: Healing with Ho'oponopono.* youtube.com, 1 Mar. 2012. Web.

[21] Brown, Brene?. *Rising Strong.* N.p.: Spiegel & Grau, 2015. Print.

[22] Bernstein, Gabrielle. "How to Accept the Things You Cannot Change." *gabbybTV.com.* May 2015. Web.

[23] *The Shift.* Dir. Micheal Goorjian. Perf. Wayne Dyer. Hay House Films, 2009.

Lightning Source UK Ltd.
Milton Keynes UK
UKHW021825030222
398153UK00009B/2257

9 780994 564603